W9-AZK-383

Gave To:

May 2002

THE INVISIBLE HAND

R.C. SPROUL

The Invisible Hand

*Do All Things Really
Work for Good?*

WORD PUBLISHING
DALLAS   LONDON   VANCOUVER   MELBOURNE

Word Publishing
1996

Book design by Mark McGarry
Set in Aldus

Library of Congress Cataloging-in-Publication Data
Sproul, R.C. (Robert Charles), 1939–
p. cm.
ISBN 0–8499–1207–5
1. Providence and government of God. 2. Good and Evil.
3. God — Will. 4. God — Goodness.   I. Title.
BT135.S75   1996   213'.5 — dc20
96–21868
CIP

Printed in the United States of America.

6 7 8 0 1 2 3 4 9   BVG   9 8 7 6 5 4 3 2 1

To Maureen and Dave Buchman,
who bring joy out of sorrow
and order out of chaos.

[Contents]

[*Acknowledgments*]

Though one of my duties as a seminary professor is to explore the doctrine of providence in an academic and technical theological fashion, I have tried to keep this book at least one step removed from the academic realm. It is written for the laity, for theirs is a concern that faces the hard questions of providence in the concrete arena of faith—and rarely from the abstract vantage point of the academic arena. At times I find it well-nigh impossible to avoid the abstract altogether. I am afraid at times I skate over the line into the academic realm. When that occurs I seek to explain and illustrate the material in a way that I trust does not demand a seminary background. Where I fail in that regard the fault is mine and not that of my excellent and helpful editor, Sue Ann Jones. Without Sue Ann's able assistance this book would have been more academic and far less readable. My thanks go to her and also to Maureen Buchman and Donna Mack for their help in preparing the manuscript. Special thanks also to Joey Paul, Kip Jordon, and Nelson Keener at Word for their gracious patience with me in this endeavor.

R. C. Sproul
Orlando, Easter 1996

ix

[*Chapter 1*]

Hard Providence

I HAD JUST PULLED MY CAR INTO THE GARAGE AND stepped out of it when the door to the kitchen opened and my daughter, Sherrie, appeared. Her face was ashen, and there was a look of horror in her eyes. She rushed into my arms, blurting out the words, "Oh, Daddy! My baby is dead!"

I held her against my chest as she sobbed and sobbed. She was in the ninth month of her pregnancy and had just returned from a checkup with her obstetrician. He could not detect a heartbeat. As gently as he could, he explained what that meant: her unborn child had died in her womb.

The following morning Sherrie was admitted to the hospital. Her doctor induced contractions, and she quickly went into labor, knowing that her child would be stillborn. The practice of the hospital in such cases is to follow through with the procedures of an otherwise normal birth. So when the baby, a beautiful little girl, was born, she was cleaned, measured, weighed, and had her footprint recorded in ink. Then the moribund child was handed to her mother. Sherrie cuddled the baby for several minutes then handed her to her husband. After a few moments I was permitted to hold my granddaughter in my arms.

1

I have found it difficult to recognize newborn infants by their facial features; they all seem to look alike to me. But the image of that tiny child was burned into my memory forever. As I held her I was overwhelmed by this incredible conjunction of life and death. The child was perfectly formed in every respect. But she was not breathing.

Sherrie and her husband, Tim, named the child Alicia. She was buried with a regular funeral service attended by our family and our pastor. We stood by the grave and wept together as we committed her body to the earth and her soul to our heavenly Father.

Every woman who has delivered a stillborn baby knows the devastation it brings to the heart. Who can experience such a thing without crying to heaven and asking, "Why?" It is normal to wonder where God is in such circumstances. It is where the rubber of human anguish meets the road of divine providence.

This book is an effort to face those issues and questions that arise with regard to God's providence. It is designed to look at the question of providence, not only from a doctrinal viewpoint, but chiefly from an examination of concrete experiences of the flesh-and-blood people whose lives and struggles are recorded for us in sacred Scripture.

One of those people was King David.

Bowing Before God's Providence

David was stricken, assaulted in his conscience by the searing words of the prophet Nathan. Those words echoed in his ears and pierced his soul: "YOU ARE THE MAN." What had begun as a report of egregious wrongdoing by a subject in his kingdom was suddenly turned on the king himself. David thought he was hearing an account of selfish exploitation by an unnamed perpetrator. He was unaware that he was listening to a thinly veiled parable of himself, a prophetic narrative aimed at the king's own conscience. It was a simple tale.

Then the LORD sent Nathan to David. And he came to him, and said to him: "There were two men in one city, one rich and the other poor. The rich man had exceedingly many flocks and herds. But the poor man had nothing, except one little ewe lamb which he had bought and nourished; and it grew up together with him and with his children. It ate of his own food and drank from his own cup and lay in his bosom; and it was like a daughter to him. And a traveler came to the rich man, who refused to take from his own flock and from his own herd to prepare one for the wayfaring man who had come to him; but he took the poor man's lamb and prepared it for the man who had come to him."

So David's anger was greatly aroused against the man, and he said to Nathan, "As the LORD lives, the man who has done this shall surely die! And he shall restore fourfold for the lamb, because he did this thing and because he had no pity."

Then Nathan said to David, "You are the man!" (2 Sam. 12:1–7)

A torrent of guilt swept over David. The parable hit home, striking his heart. His eyes were opened as he suddenly saw the truth about himself he had been so careful to conceal. This was David, the one who was known as a man after God's own heart. This was the champion of Israel, her greatest warrior. This was Israel's most illustrious king, the author of the psalms. He had ascended to the throne at the death of Saul, whom God had rejected as king over Israel. David was the Lord's anointed one who was elevated after the mighty had fallen. He rued the disgrace of Saul and chafed at the triumphalism of the Philistines who would publish the news in Gath and whose troubadours would gleefully sing, "O how the mighty have fallen."

Now David had joined the ranks of the fallen. His fall was great and is recorded for all posterity. He was a living Shakespearean-style hero marred by a fatal blemish, marked with an indelible scandal.

David's fall began with a simple thought, an inclination born of lust when he inadvertently spied a beautiful woman at her bath. He

3

didn't start out with a scheme to commit adultery. He was not on the prowl for the first available paramour. One moment of lust had exploded into a compulsive passion. Then David threw righteousness to the wind and gambled his soul in exchange for illicit romance. He put his conscience on hold and hardened his own heart. The biblical record is as revealing of the heart of darkness that lurks in the chest of every man as it is terse:

> Then it happened one evening that David arose from his bed and walked on the roof of the king's house. And from the roof he saw a woman bathing, and the woman was very beautiful to behold. So David sent and inquired about the woman. And someone said, "Is this not Bathsheba, the daughter of Eliam, the wife of Uriah the Hittite?" Then David sent messengers, and took her; and she came to him, and he lay with her, for she was cleansed from her impurity; and she returned to her house. (2 Sam. 11:2–4)

David took another man's wife. Like the rich man in Nathan's parable, David helped himself to the ewe lamb of one of his trusted soldiers. Uriah was married to Bathsheba. Yet while Uriah was serving David with loyalty, David was taking liberties with Uriah's wife. Bathsheba became pregnant, and the child in her womb was not, indeed could not have been, fathered by Uriah.

Obviously panic seized David's heart. He plotted an elaborate scheme to cover up his sin. He decided to grant Uriah a furlough from battle, a respite from war so that he could return for a season to his home and to his wife. This way when the child would be born Uriah could be deceived into thinking that it was his. David heaped the praise of hypocrisy upon Uriah, gave him a gift (obviously designed to soothe David's conscience), and sent him home.

But David underestimated Uriah's loyalty. Uriah was not willing to abandon his post or take advantage of the king's generosity. He was a soldier. No matter how great was his longing to be with his wife, he still felt constrained to give service to his king. Instead of returning home as David had planned . . .

Uriah slept at the door of the king's house with all the servants of his lord, and did not go down to his house. So when they told David, saying, "Uriah did not go down to his house," David said to Uriah, "Did you not come from a journey? Why did you not go down to your house?"

And Uriah said to David, "The ark and Israel and Judah are dwelling in tents, and my lord Joab and the servants of my lord are encamped in the open fields. Shall I then go to my house to eat and drink, and to lie with my wife? As you live, and as your soul lives, I will not do this thing."

Then David said to Uriah, "Wait here today also, and tomorrow I will let you depart." So Uriah remained in Jerusalem that day and the next. Now when David called him, he ate and drank before him; and he made him drunk. And at evening he went out to lie on his bed with the servants of his lord, but he did not go down to his house. (2 Sam. 11:9–13)

David's scheme was thwarted. His desperate plan of cover-up was frustrated by the loyalty of the very man he had betrayed. At this point one might expect that David would have been awakened from his lustful slumber and would have been led to contrition. On the contrary! With growing desperation David added sin to sin and compounded his guilt with virtual murder. He wrote his general, Joab, a letter that would be revealed to all history by the secret operation of God the Holy Spirit. No shredding machine was available to destroy this evidence and conceal it from public scrutiny. David stooped to the nadir of nefarious conduct by having Uriah himself carry the sealed letter to Joab. In his naive loyalty, Uriah had no idea that the missive he carried to the front contained his own death warrant:

And he wrote in the letter, saying, "Set Uriah in the forefront of the hottest battle, and retreat from him, that he may be struck down and die." So it was, while Joab besieged the city, that he assigned Uriah to a place where he knew there were valiant men. Then the men of the city came out and fought with Joab. And some of the people of the servants of David fell; and Uriah the Hittite died also. (2 Sam. 11:15–17)

Later a messenger was sent by Joab from the scene of battle to inform David that Uriah had been slain. David thought he was safe, that his secret was hidden from the eyes of men, buried with the body of Uriah. Bathsheba also received the report and immediately went into mourning. But not for long. When David sent for her she went to his house, became his wife, and bore him a son. It seemed that no one would ever know that the child born to them was the son of adultery.

But the God of all providence had his eye upon David. The king's secret did not elude His gaze. What was hidden from human discernment was naked before Him. In classic understatement Scripture says: "But the thing that David had done displeased the LORD" (2 Sam. 11:27b).

It was that divine displeasure that prompted the visit of Nathan to David. Nathan was burdened with the weight of the truth of the matter. His task was onerous as he was sent by God to confront a king. That is dangerous business for a prophet, as the experiences of Elijah and John the Baptist well attest. Yet the response of David to prophetic judgment was quite unlike that of Ahab or Herod. David heard the prophet's word and was broken by it. After the bold declaration that David was the man of the parable, God spoke His full indictment against David through the lips of the prophet Nathan:

Then Nathan said to David, "You are the man! Thus says the LORD God of Israel: 'I anointed you king over Israel, and I delivered you from the hand of Saul. I gave you your master's house and your master's wives into your keeping, and gave you the house of Israel and Judah. And if that had been too little, I also would have given you much more! Why have you despised the commandment of the LORD, to do evil in His sight? You have killed Uriah the Hittite with the sword; you have taken his wife to be your wife, and have killed him with the sword of the people of Ammon. Now therefore, the sword shall never depart from your house, because you have despised Me, and have taken the wife of Uriah the Hittite to be your wife.' Thus says the LORD: 'Behold, I will raise up adversity against you from your own house; and I will take your wives before your eyes and give them to your neighbor, and he shall lie with your wives in the sight of this sun. For you did it secretly, but I will do this thing before all Israel, before the sun.'" (2 Sam. 12:7–11)

In the indictment God rehearsed the blessings He had bestowed upon David. All that David had received he had received from the invisible hand of God's providence. The blessing of that providence was now to be followed by judgment. The hand of God was heavy upon David. Yet the hand was not so heavy that it did not hold grace as well as judgment. Even here the justice of God was being tempered by mercy. God could have invoked the death penalty on David. David's offenses were capital crimes in Israel.

The heart of David melted. His response was that of deep and genuine repentance. His was no attrition born of a fear of punishment; his was contrition, a true remorse for having offended God. In his epic psalm of repentance following this incident, David cried out, "Against You, You only, have I sinned and done this evil in Your sight" (Ps. 51:4). This statement must be taken as hyperbole as it is not strictly accurate. David did more than sin against God. He sinned against Uriah; he sinned against Bathsheba; he sinned against his own family; he sinned against the whole nation, betraying its confidence in him as king. Yet ultimately all sin is against God and, in ultimate terms, *only* against Him, though in a proximate sense it involved others.

To Nathan, David replied before he wrote his lengthy penitential psalm: "I have sinned against the LORD" (2 Sam. 12:13). David's confession of sin, his acknowledgment of his guilt without any attempts at self-justification, was immediately met with the announcement of God's pardon:

7

So David said to Nathan, "I have sinned against the LORD."

And Nathan said to David, "The LORD also has put away your sin; you shall not die. However, because by this deed you have given great occasion to the enemies of the LORD to blaspheme, the child also who is born to you shall surely die." (2 Sam. 12:13–14)

The Scope of God's Providence

God put away the sin of David. This meant that God was granting remission to David for his sins. But though the eternal guilt of David's sin was remitted he still received temporal punishment for his sin. Through Nathan God announced that the child of the adulterous union would be taken from David and Bathsheba. What follows is a difficult verse to assimilate into our faith but one that bears heavily upon our understanding of the providence of God:

Then Nathan departed to his house.

And the LORD struck the child that Uriah's wife bore to David, and it became ill. (2 Sam. 12:15)

Scripture declares that the Lord struck the infant child of David with a mortal illness. This is a hard saying. It is commonplace in the church today to hear vain attempts by preachers to exonerate God from any involvement in human sickness and death. I heard one televangelist declare that God has nothing to do with disease and death. He assigned these human tragedies to the work of Satan.

Such sentiments do violence, not only to our understanding of the providence of God, but to our understanding of the whole character of God. Christianity is not a religion of dualism by which God and Satan are equal and opposite opposing forces destined to fight an eternal struggle that must result in a tie. God is sovereign over His entire creation, including the subordinate domain of Satan. God is Lord of death as well as life. He rules over pain and disease as sovereignly as He rules over prosperity.

If God had nothing to do with sickness or death, Christians, of all people, would be the most to be pitied. It would mean living in a universe ruled by chaos where our Father's hand was tied by fate and bound by the fickleness of chance. His arm would not be mighty to save; it would be impotent. But, the preachers to the contrary, God has everything to do with sickness and death. God majors in suffering. The way of redemption is the *Via Dolorosa*, the road to the cross. Our Lord was Himself a man of sorrows and acquainted with grief. No, God is not removed from or aloof from human suffering; it is contained within the scope of His providence. Our family understood that truth when Sherrie and her husband lost their baby.

And David also understood these things, as is seen by the subsequent narrative:

David therefore pleaded with God for the child, and David fasted and went in and lay all night on the ground. So the elders of his house arose and went to him, to raise him up from the ground. But he would not, nor did he eat food with them. Then on the seventh day it came to pass that the child died. And the servants of David were afraid to tell him that the child was dead. For they said, "Indeed, while the child was alive, we spoke to him, and he would not heed our voice. How can we tell him that the child is dead? He may do some harm!"

When David saw that his servants were whispering, David perceived that the child was dead. Therefore David said to his servants, "Is the child dead?"

And they said, "He is dead."

So David arose from the ground, washed and anointed himself, and changed his clothes; and he went into the house of the LORD and worshiped. Then he went to his own house; and when he requested, they set food before him, and he ate. Then his servants said to him, "What is this that you have done? You fasted and wept for the child while he was alive, but when the child died, you arose and ate food."

And he said, "While the child was alive, I fasted and wept; for I said, 'Who can tell whether the LORD will be gracious to me, that the child may live?' But now he is dead; why should I fast? Can I bring him back again? I shall go to him, but he shall not return to me." (2 Sam. 12:16–23)

For seven days David wrestled with God. He prayed and fasted and refused to be comforted. His servants were deeply concerned that their king would do harm to himself. They pled with David to give it up, to eat and care for himself. When the child died they were terrified to report it to David. But David was astute. He deduced from their whispers that the child had perished. Then, when he elicited the truth from them, he did something that amazed the servants. David got up, washed, anointed himself, and went to the house of God to worship Him.

Here we encounter the David who was a man after God's own heart. Here the character that resonates throughout the psalms makes himself clear. When God said no to the pleas of David, he immediately went to church—not to whine or complain but to worship. Here we see David living *coram Deo*, before the face of God. David pled his case before the throne of the Almighty—and lost. Yet he was willing to bow before the providence of God, to let God be God.

Such acquiescence before the providence of God is difficult for the world to understand. David's servants failed to grasp it; they saw in their king a spiritual anomaly. His behavior made no sense to them. They sought to rebuke him for his topsy-turvy actions. They thought David should have been in mourning *after* the child had died, believing that was the time for sackcloth and ashes, not while the child was still alive.

When David explained himself to his servants he gave them a lesson in the doctrine of providence. Though David had clearly heard God's declaration that the child would die and he did not regard it as an idle threat, he was also aware of God's actions in the past when He had relented from promised judgments when the people turned to Him in repentance.

David explained his entreaties by saying, "Who can tell whether the LORD will be gracious to me, that the child may live?" The phrase "who can tell?" is the key to understanding David's prolonged fast and importunate prayer. The "who can tell?" calls attention to the *Deus absconditus*, the "hidden God" whose secret counsel remains unknown to us. David had heard the words of the *Deus revelatus*, the "revealed" God, but held out hope that it was not the entire story. When he discovered that God had not held any of His plan in reserve it was enough to satisfy his soul and submit to God's "no." In a sense David's struggle foreshadowed something of the agony of Christ in Gethsemane as Jesus wrestled with the revealed will of the Father, but in the final analysis was willing to drink of the cup to its fullest measure.

If we understand the providence of God and love the God of providence, we are able to worship Him with the sacrifice of praise He inherently deserves when things occur that bring pain, sorrow, and affliction into our lives. This understanding of providence is vital to all who would worship God. It is a worship of faith that is rooted in trust. David trusted God for his own future, and he trusted God for the future of his son. David realized he had not yet heard the rest of the story and that all the subsequent chapters would be written by God.

Chapter 2

The Invisible Hand

THE WORD "PROVIDENCE" HAS ALL BUT DISAPPEARED FROM the vocabulary of the contemporary Christian. It is becoming obsolete and archaic. This word that once was commonplace, indeed central to Christian expression, now seems doomed to the ash heap of useful verbiage.

In the early nineties a television documentary on the Civil War gripped the interest of the nation as the drama of America's bloodiest conflict was retold. Excerpts from letters written home by soldiers of both North and South were replete with references to "Providence." On the eve of battle soldiers wrote to their wives or parents about their fears and of the uncertainty of what would happen to them on the morrow and spoke often of their lives being in the hands of Providence. The term *Providence* was capitalized as it referred not so much to the rule of God over the affairs of men, but to God Himself. The term *Providence* became a title for the deity.

This link between the *activity* of God and the very *being* of God was deeply rooted in the conviction of nineteenth-century Christians that all that comes to pass occurs under the sovereign plan and rule of almighty God. There was a constant sense that all of life was lived *coram Deo,* before the face of God.

Now this attitude has changed. The culture in which we presently live has little room for thoughts of God's providence. At best we live in a modern climate of neo-deism; at worst the culture is defined by a climate of neo-paganism. The prevailing assumption of our day is that we live in a closed, mechanistic universe where events occur either by fixed, impersonal laws of impersonal forces—or merely by chance. It is the age of secularism, where there appears to be no access to the transcendent or the supernatural. Nature is viewed as being strictly natural. Religion, if it is tolerated at all, is relegated to an isolated compartment, a reservation with strictly defined borders. People may still indulge in religious activity for purposes of personal well-being and psychological fulfillment, but religion has no relevant role in the public square or in serious reflections about the nature of the cosmos or the course of world history. The God of Christianity is in exile. Nobody thinks of naming a newly incorporated village or city "Providence," as was once deemed appropriate in Rhode Island.

Modern fads in religion, including the resurgence of Gnostic belief systems in New Age thinking, the fascination with the occult, and the preoccupation with angels and demons in some sectors may be seen as desperate attempts by modern people to break out of the rigid enclosure of the prevailing view of the universe. That every daily newspaper includes a horoscope and that New Age book and gift stores are proliferating all over the country are indicators of this desperate exercise in futility. A profound sense of the absence of God evokes these neo-mythological stabs toward transcendence.

In the eighteenth century Adam Smith wrote his classic work *The Wealth of Nations* in which he sought to apply the scientific method to the vagaries of economic enterprises and discover the laws that govern economics. Smith was searching for the "invisible hand" of Providence. In our time that invisible hand is not merely deemed invisible but nonexistent. The hand of Providence has been chopped off altogether, and with that amputation we are left to grope alone in a hostile or, even worse, an indifferent universe. We look no more to the invisible hand of Providence for our economic well-being but to the highly visible hand of human government to solve these questions.

Words have a nasty habit of slipping in and out of vogue. One generation's pet phrases are seen as "out of it" by later generations. In the forties the standard response to a good experience was summed up by the word *swell.* It seemed to exhaust the vocabulary of Hollywood's Van Johnson in his wartime repartee with June Allyson. But "swell" soon gave way to "cool" or "groovy" or "neat." Trying to keep up with teenage nomenclature is an impossible mission for the aging adult. The phrases and words change too rapidly for us, and we merely sound foolish trying to keep up. As soon as we try to speak to teenagers in their own language, we see the smirks on their faces when they catch us using a word that is suddenly "out."

But the word *providence* is too rich and too heavily loaded with crucial theological nuance to allow it to pass from our language without a fight. It is not a slang term fit for a specific generation but a term with centuries, indeed millennia, of historic significance. It is a theological term of the highest import, a term rooted in the ageless content of Scripture itself.

A Matter of Confidence

The word *providence* is derived from a Latin prefix and root. The prefix *pro* indicates "before" or "in front of." The basic root comes from the Latin *videre,* which means "to see." This root still figures prominently in current language as we are a culture highly influenced by the phenomenon of television. When we put the prefix and the root together we have a word that means "to see beforehand," so we might be tempted to conclude that *providence* simply refers to the foreknowledge, or prescience, of God. But although the concept of providence includes some reference to God's foreknowledge, it is by no means exhausted by this idea. *Providence* is not merely a synonym for *foreknowledge*. Rather, the concept of providence is multifaceted and includes a wide range of divine activities, as I shall attempt to demonstrate.

In the first instance, the word *providence* refers to God's *provision* for His people. We use the word *provisions* to refer to things we acquire for future needs and exigencies. I do not know what tomorrow will hold for me or for my family, so I take certain steps today to provide for tomorrow. When the weather channel warns of tropical storms and hurricanes that threaten our part of Florida, my wife fills the bathtub with water and stocks up with foodstuffs and other supplies. I have met with my attorney and drawn up a will to make provisions for my wife and children in the event of my death.

Yet with all the provisions I seek to make for my family's future, I realize that ultimately their well-being is in the hands of God. I look to Him as the Great Provider for them as well as for myself. I do not control my destiny or that of my family. This is not my world; it is my Father's world. I do not entrust my family to Allstate; there are better hands than theirs. I take seriously the admonition of Jesus:

"Therefore I say to you, do not worry about your life, what you will eat or what you will drink; nor about your body, what you will put on. Is not life more than food and the body more than clothing? Look at the birds of the air, for they neither sow nor reap nor gather into barns; yet your heavenly Father feeds them. Are you not of more value than they? Which of you by worrying can add one cubit to his stature?

"So why do you worry about clothing? Consider the lilies of the field, how they grow: they neither toil nor spin; and yet I say to you that even Solomon in all his glory was not arrayed like one of these. Now if God so clothes the grass of the field, which today is, and tomorrow is thrown into the oven, will He not much more clothe you, O you of little faith?

"Therefore do not worry, saying, 'What shall we eat?' or 'What shall we drink?' or 'What shall we wear?' For after all these things the Gentiles seek. For your heavenly Father knows that you need all these things. But seek first the kingdom of God and His righteousness, and all these things shall be added to you. Therefore do not worry about tomorrow, for tomorrow will worry about its own things. Sufficient for the day is its own trouble." (Matt. 6:25–34)

These words of Jesus do not prohibit the exercise of responsible stewardship. They are designed to be a lesson on anxiety. We are not to be frantic about our future needs. We are not to live in the bondage of worry. Our worry and anxiety are to be assuaged by our confidence in the providence of God. The lily has no need for worry beads or the psychiatrist's couch.

It is a matter of focus. If we are diligent in our quest for the kingdom of God and His righteousness, our concern for earthly provisions will be clearly met. As David said, "I have been young, and now am old; Yet I have not seen the righteous forsaken, nor his descendants begging bread" (Ps. 37:25).

Jesus' teaching in the Sermon on the Mount calls attention to the providence of God. He speaks of the birds of the air who are fed by the hand of Providence, and He insists that we are of more value than birds. The point of the comparison is in the concept of "much more." God places a premium of value on the welfare of His children that exceeds the value of the animal kingdom. Yet His providential care extends to both. Not only does He number the hairs on our heads but He notices the fall of every sparrow. As the song declares, "His eye is on the sparrow . . . but He also watches us."

Because the word *providence* is rooted in the Latin term for seeing or vision, we may be tempted to restrict its theological application to God's mere observance of human activity. It is not merely that God looks at human affairs. The point is that He looks *after* human affairs. He not only watches us, He watches *over* us. The child's most simple prayer is, "Please watch over Mommy, Daddy, Grandma," etc.

It is the watching over us that goes to the heart of divine providence. It is God's fatherly care of His creatures that the word *provi-dence* encompasses. This means God is *involved* in human affairs. He is not like Aristotle's god, the Unmoved Mover, who remains aloof and totally uninvolved with human history. Will Durant once compared Aristotle's god with the monarch of England, whom he described as a "do-nothing king who reigns but doesn't rule." The biblical God is not unmoved. He is a moved and moving Mover who rules as well as reigns.

The God of deism and neo-deism is more like the god of Aristotle, a supreme clockmaker who designs and fashions an intricate clock, winds it up, and then steps out of the picture and lets it run by itself. This view regards the laws of nature as laws that operate somewhat independently from divine providence, allowing for no intrusion from on high. These laws are fixed and mechanical. In contrast the Christian faith allows for natural laws but sees these laws as the law of God, always subject to His sovereign rule. They reflect the normal or ordinary way in which God governs His universe.

Divine Sustenance

Making provisions for things has to do with the providing of sustenance. Sustenance is what is required to keep things going or to keep them alive. The ancient Hebrew looked to the benediction of God whereby God would not only bless His people but also *keep* them. This benediction was deeply concerned with the preservation of His people. In a word, it focused on the *sustaining* of His people.

Divine sustenance is tied to the biblical concept of creation. The opening words of the Bible say, "In the beginning God created the heavens and the earth" (Gen. 1:1). The Hebrew word for "create" is the word *bara*. Built into this concept of *bara* is the notion of sustenance.

We may look to the realm of music for an analogy. We know the sound of a staccato note: short, brief, and abrupt, like the sound *beep!* In contrast if the tone is sustained it is elongated and drawn out: *beeeeeeeeeep.* We can strike a note on the piano and hold the pedal down to sustain the sound. Similarly, God's work of Creation is not a staccato action; what God creates He sustains. He not only brings things into being out of nothing, He keeps them in existence. The usual biblical term for this is to *uphold.*

> God, who at various times and in various ways spoke in time past to the fathers by the prophets, has in these last days spoken to us by His Son, whom He has appointed heir of all things, through whom also He made the worlds; who being the brightness of His glory and the express image of His person, and upholding all things by the word of His power, when He had by Himself purged our sins, sat down at the right hand of the Majesty on high. (Heb. 1:1–3)

In this text the reference to Christ is to the One who *upholds* "all things by the word of His power."

The Westminster Confession of Faith defines the providence of God as follows:

> God the great Creator of all things doth uphold, direct, dispose, and govern all creatures, actions, and things, from the greatest even to the least, by his most wise and holy providence, according to his infallible foreknowledge, and the free and immutable counsel of his own will, to the praise of the glory of his wisdom, power, justice, goodness, and mercy. (v/1)

This confessional definition refers to several aspects of God's providence. We will elaborate more fully on these various aspects later. For now we will focus on the first assertion of the work of the Creator, namely on His work of upholding His creation. We note that this upholding refers to all creatures, actions, and things, from the greatest even to the least. This refers to the *scope* of the sustenance of divine providence, which extends to and includes everything that is. It is not that God is merely interested in the "big picture." His management of His creation is micromanagement, concerned with and involved with the smallest details.

The confession indicates that God's providential upholding of all things is "by his most wise and holy providence." The word *by* in this phrase indicates the means by which God sustains what He upholds. Here the means are rooted in His wisdom and holiness. We must not pass too glibly over these adjectival qualifiers. God's work of upholding His creation is grounded in His wisdom. As mortals we are prone to mistakes in holding on to things either for too short a period or too long a time. What speculator in the stock market has never sold too early or purchased too late? God makes no mistakes in His holdings. He sustains whatsoever He sustains to a perfect degree precisely because He upholds according to His perfect wisdom.

The upholding work of God is also a holy sustaining. In this regard the term *holy* refers both to His transcendent majesty and to His perfect righteousness. There is no flaw of intelligence, wisdom, or righteousness in His work of sustenance. What God keeps, He keeps righteously. At times we wonder about the duration of pain and affliction and ask, "How long, O God, must we endure these things?" We wonder why God allows evil to go on unchecked. Yet the duration of all things is in His hands, and their time span is controlled by His providence according to His wisdom and according to His holy purpose.

We also note that God sustains things according to His foreknowledge, which the confession reminds us is infallible. God does not indulge in guesswork in His prognostications. He does not consult a tote board to figure the odds. His foreknowledge is both infallible and absolute. There is nothing in the future that He does not already know. He knows the end from the very beginning. It is said that God knows all future contingencies yet He does not know them *contingently*. That is, if we were to ask God about some future possibility, He would never answer us by saying, "That depends."

From our creaturely perspective we regard the future in terms of

contingencies. We have a plan B in case our plan A fails to material-
ize. To the finite mind, future events appear contingent. That is
because we are contingent beings, dependent upon something outside ourselves for our very existence. But God is not a dependent or
contingent Being. He knows what He knows absolutely. He foreknows what He foreknows because what He foreknows He also
forewills. We are instructed by Scripture to bracket our statements
about the future by saying *"Deo Volente"* (God willing). God does
not have to speak in those terms because He is the *Deo* of the *Deo
Volente.*

God upholds all things by the free and immutable counsel of His
own will. This is important to grasp. The sustaining providence of
God is driven by His will, and His will is absolutely free. It is bound
and determined by no creaturely thing. It is not subject to our
whims or actions. His will is not only free but immutably so.
Nothing can change His freedom or suddenly arise to block it. His
counsel remains forever. He does not change His mind because He
receives new information or needs to correct an error. He has an
eternal plan that contains no defects. There is no plan B for God.
His counsel is immutable because He is immutable in all that He
is. His omniscience does not change. His omnipotence never weak-
ens. His wisdom never falters. His memory never fails. There are
no mutations in the divine being or character.

The Highest Possible Good

To what end or purpose does God uphold all things? It is to the
praise of His glory. This is a difficult concept to embrace in full
measure because it suggests a kind of self-centeredness in God,
and we are taught to see self-centeredness as sin. Indeed, to be
self-centered is a sin for any creature. We mortals are called to be
God-centered in our thinking. For creatures, God-centeredness is a
virtue, and self-centeredness a vice. But for God, self-centeredness
is pure virtue because it is also God-centeredness. For us to be God-

centered is to fix our attention upon the most perfect Being. So it is for God Himself.

Though what God does in His providence benefits us, its highest virtue is found in its glorification of God Himself. God's upholding of His creation reflects upon His own glory, and that glory is not a divine vice but is the highest possible good. If God were centered on something less than Himself, that focus would reflect a defect in Himself and render Him less than God and unworthy of our worship.

It is a sweet and excellent paradox that God's provision for His creatures and His upholding of His creation is also the manifestation of His eternal glory.

Calvin remarked about this when he wrote:

> First, then, let the reader remember that the providence we mean is not one by which the Deity, sitting idly in heaven, looks on at what is taking place in the world, but one by which he, as it were, holds the helm, and overrules all events. Hence his providence extends not less to the hand than to the eye. That is to say, he not only sees, but ordains what he wills to be done. (*Institutes*, 175)

In these works of Providence the glory of His wisdom, power, justice, goodness, and mercy is made manifest.

Chapter 3

Providence as Provision

"SO ABRAHAM ROSE EARLY IN THE MORNING . . ." (GEN. 22:3).
This terse, almost innocuous statement referring to Abraham's
time of arousal from sleep has been the subject of much speculation. Why did Abraham arise early on this day when he was to
commit, at God's command, a most horrendous deed?

The Danish philosopher Soren Kierkegaard wrote a book entitled
Fear and Trembling in which he turned this phrase over and over,
trying to guess why the patriarch rose up early. Was it because he
was eager and willing to be prompt in obeying God in the task He
had set before him? Was it because the terms of his call from God
were so troubling to his soul that his sleep was filled with torment,
making further attempts at slumber impossible?

Scripture does not answer these questions. We are left to use our
own imaginations. I suspect, however, that Abraham's early rising
had more to do with torment than eagerness to serve. Abraham was
not a paper saint. He had feelings common to our humanity, and
the thing God had commanded him to do would surely strike terror
into the soul of any mortal. God had required of Abraham what
Kierkegaard called the "temporary suspension of the ethical." He
had summoned Abraham to commit murder—and not just any

ordinary act of homicide. God had ordered Abraham to kill his own son.

It is true that this command to Abraham was given before the Decalogue, the Ten Commandments, were given to Moses on Mount Sinai. The Law had not yet been delivered on tablets of stone. So it was not yet written, "Thou shalt not kill." But before it was uttered in the special revelation of Sinai it was already inscribed by nature in the hearts of men. Long before Moses was born, Cain already knew that in the order of creation it was a heinous crime to kill his brother. The scream of Able's blood was heard down through the centuries. That murder was a capital offense, a crime against God Himself because an assault against human life was an assault against an image bearer of God, was clearly revealed to Noah and his progeny.

No, Abraham had to know that murder was in violent opposition to the law of God, and yet he had heard the words of God directly and clearly, words that went against everything he knew about the character of the God whom later generations would revere as the very God of Abraham. The words were part of one of the most difficult tests God would ever impose upon a human being. We read of this test in Genesis 22:

> Now it came to pass after these things that God tested Abraham, and said to him, "Abraham!"
> And he said, "Here I am."
> And He said, "Take now your son, your only son Isaac, whom you love, and go to the land of Moriah, and offer him there as a burnt offering on one of the mountains of which I shall tell you." (Gen. 22:1–2)

Much is contained in this terse summary of a poignant event in the life of Abraham. God called him to a test; indeed for Abraham it was the supreme test. Abraham's life to this point had been marked by an extraordinary level of trust. This is the man who had left his homeland and all that he held dear to travel to an unknown country at the summons of a strange and foreign God. This God had made an astonishing promise to him and sealed this promise with a sacred covenant. God had promised Abraham in his old age that he would become the father of a great nation and that his descendants would be as the stars of the sky and the sands of the sea.

The promise came to Abraham when his wife, Sarah, was aged and barren. Yet Abraham believed God and hoped against hope that the promise would someday be fulfilled and that his heir would not be his servant Eliezer of Damascus but a son from his own loins, flesh of his flesh and bone of his bone.

To be sure, Abraham had taken steps of his own to ensure that the promise would be fulfilled; he had fathered a child from his wife's handmaiden, Hagar. This son was Ishmael, who was not the child of promise. Nor was the promise quickly fulfilled. Abraham waited for years for his wife to conceive. She had laughed at the very idea that she would ever bear a child. She remembered her laughter when she did in fact bear a son; the child was named Isaac, which meant "laughter."

When Isaac was born, Abraham beheld the flesh-and-blood fulfillment of God's promise to him. The impossible dream was realized, and the seed of the covenant promise was alive and well. Now Abraham faced the test of all tests when God demanded that Abraham put the child of promise to death.

We note that the terms of God's command were painfully specific. He did not simply order Abraham to "kill your son." Had the command been that unspecific we would have expected Abraham to go directly to Ishmael and offer him upon the altar of sacrifice. Rather, God left nothing to ambiguity. He ordered Abraham to take the son he loved. To leave absolutely no doubt about who was to be slain, God said: "Take now your son, your only son Isaac, whom you love. . . ." If it had been Ishmael who had been named, perhaps Abraham could have understood. But Isaac? Isaac was, in a real sense, his *only* son. Surely he was the son Abraham loved more than he loved life itself. There was nothing more precious to him than Isaac. But it was Isaac, the child of promise, the sole hope of

Abraham's future progeny, who was named for the sacrifice on Mount Moriah.

It was after this blood-curdling commandment that Abraham rose up early in the morning. The scriptural narrative continues:

> So Abraham rose early in the morning and saddled his donkey, and took two of his young men with him, and Isaac his son; and he split the wood for the burnt offering, and arose and went to the place of which God had told him. (Gen. 22:3)

The details of the story are surprising. We are told that after he rose early Abraham proceeded to saddle his donkey. I wonder about this detail. Abraham was one of the wealthiest men of his era. He had a multitude of servants at his beck and call. He was also aged. I would not expect this old and wealthy man to be engaged in such a menial task as putting a saddle on a donkey. Yet Abraham attended to this task alone.

We are also told that he personally split the wood that would be used in the burnt offering. This action borders on the macabre. Was this an exercise in masochism? What on earth was going on inside his mind while he was chopping the wood? Was he seeking some catharsis with this physical labor, as Martin Luther once observed about himself? He said that when he was stricken with a fit of melancholy or besieged by an assault of depression he would turn his attention to some physical task to get his mind off whatever was troubling him.

I once had a piano teacher whose infant granddaughter died when she got into her father's medical bag (her father was a medical missionary) and ingested a fatal dose of pills. My piano teacher was grief-stricken by the death of the child. She told me she sought solace at the piano because she could feel her grief moving out of her soul through her fingers and into the keyboard. Perhaps the ax was Abraham's keyboard, a physical conduit to release his intense emotion of the morning. With every swing of the ax, his blinding pain was being released into the wood.

When the preparatory tasks were completed, Abraham arose once more and set out to the place where God commanded. As his greater Son would do centuries later, the patriarch set his face like a flint to the mountain of destiny. The journey surely was made all the more grievous by the distance and time it required. It was not as if Abraham could finish the deed quickly. He had time to think about what lay ahead.

I find it difficult, if not impossible, to get inside the head of Abraham on his journey to Mount Moriah. I have never had the experience of being called to slay my son for the glory of God. The closest thing to it in my own experience pales into insignificance by comparison. It occurred not with my son, but with my dog.

When I began Ligonier Ministries in 1971 I was given a special gift of two German shepherd puppies by the benefactress of our work. Mrs. Dora Hillman gave our family two puppies that had been born on Palm Sunday. She named them Hallelujah and Hosannah. Hallie was the female, and Hosie the male. They were bred of champion stock; the sire of the litter was the Canadian Grand Victor, and the brood bitch was the champion of the noted Mellon family of Pittsburgh. Hosie was an especially magnificent animal, a classic sable German shepherd.

When Hosie was two months old he came into the kitchen through the doggie door one morning with his head swollen to almost twice its normal size. He was staggering and obviously disoriented. I quickly assumed that somehow he had encountered a bees' nest and had suffered multiple stings to his head. I rushed him to the veterinarian's office for treatment. When the vet examined him he discovered three deep fang wounds to his head that had obviously been made by a poisonous snake, either a copperhead or rattlesnake. The snake had injected enough venom to be fatal to the young dog. The vet declared that it was the worst case of snakebite he had ever seen in an animal, and he gave me a grim prognosis. He explained that the ability for poisonous snakes to kill was vastly overrated and that the potency of their strikes depended upon several factors including the physical size of the animal stricken, the area of the body where the venom was injected, and the amount of venom the snake injected. On all these counts the puppy was in serious danger. The vet went on to explain that Hosie would have to go through some serious crisis stages in order to survive.

The first crisis was to survive the initial shock and the impact of the venom itself. The second was the crisis provoked by the severe swelling. He said that when animals' eyes are swollen shut and they are reduced to temporary blindness, they simply seem to lose their will to live. He explained secondary reactions that also could prove fatal.

He administered antivenom shots and other medications and told me the next forty-eight hours would be critical. Two days later the vet phoned to inform me that Hosie had survived the initial crisis stage but that he would have to remain in the vet hospital for two weeks. After that period elapsed the vet called again to report that Hosie was sufficiently recovered to come home. I was enormously relieved by the news.

The vet then issued one caveat. He told me that a secondary reaction to such episodes of poisoning was necrosis of the skin tissue affected by the bite. He explained that the poison had killed this tissue, causing it to rot and literally fall from the dog's face. He said I must be prepared for a ghastly sight because the dog's face was horribly and permanently disfigured.

All of the warnings uttered by the vet did not adequately prepare me for the sight of my dog. When I arrived at the hospital to recover Hosie, I found a dog whose facial tissue had rotted to such a degree that the skin covering his face had fallen off. I looked at naked sinew and tissue that reeked of the foul odor of rotting flesh. I scooped up the dog in my arms and placed him on the seat of my car to take him home. The vet handed me a large jar filled with a special ointment that I was required to apply to Hosie's face twice a day for weeks to come to facilitate the healing of the skin tissue. He also gave me a pair of surgical gloves to wear while applying the ointment.

When I arrived home with the dog I prepared a special bed for him in the garage. The odor from the putrefied flesh was too intense to bring Hosie into the house. Then I set upon the task of applying the first round of ointment to his face. It was an unforgettable experience as I felt a deep revulsion within myself at even coming near the animal, let alone touching this face that was oozing with all sorts of ghastly stuff. It was as if the dog could sense my apprehension or revulsion as he seemed to cower before me in canine embarrassment. This was no longer a proud young German shepherd of champion stock and extraordinary beauty. He was a pitiable specimen to behold, and I wondered if it wouldn't have been better for all concerned, especially Hosie, if he would have died from the initial impact of the poison.

I realize that it may seem a bit maudlin to explain the visceral feelings that transpired as I knelt beside Hosie for the first application of the ointment, but those feelings were quite vivid at the time. I put on the surgical gloves, held my breath against the stench, and forced myself to touch the hideous face in front of me. As I did, some undeniable communication took place between man and animal. It was a moment of pathos and tenderness. It was as if the dog understood my difficulty in giving him this care. I could see it in his eyes. If dogs have souls then Hosie's eyes were the windows to his heart. A vital bonding of love took place when I touched his skin with glove-covered hands. It was obvious and instantaneous that the ointment was soothing to him. The bonding of that moment was such that it was the last time I ever wore gloves to apply the ointment. Thereafter I applied the ointment to his face twice a day with my bare hands with absolutely no sense of revulsion.

As the days and weeks passed, Hosie was restored to health and returned to life inside the house. His face became covered over again, not with normal skin, but with hard, leathery scar tissue. With the development of the scar tissue his face looked like it was frozen into what most people described as a snarl but I preferred to consider a smile.

Hosie grew to full strength. As an adult he weighed close to one hundred pounds and had a barrel chest and an unusually docile disposition. He became my inseparable companion. When I lectured he would sleep next to the podium. Along with his mate Hallie, he produced fine litters of puppies, some of which were trained for service in the canine corps of the state police.

Hosie loved to go hunting with me in the forests of the Allegheny Mountains as we sought out ruffed grouse. On one occasion when I was hunting alone with Hosie I came to a barbed-wire fence that blocked my path. According to hunter safety I carefully slid my rifle under the fence before I tried to cross it myself. As I started to climb over the fence my wool coat got caught in the barbs. I struggled to free myself, making the wire taut, which then flipped me head over heels over the fence. I landed hard on a rock pile, my back striking a sharp rock, leaving me stunned and temporarily paralyzed. I was immobile upon the rocks. Hosie instantly sensed my predicament, and in Lassie-like heroics he snuggled his snoot under my arms so I could grasp his strong neck. I held on to him as he dragged me from the rock pile. Moments later feeling returned to my torso, and I was able to stand and walk home safely.

Two years later Hosie went into a sudden convulsion in our kitchen. I took him to the vet, who administered medication, but the medication failed to provide sustained relief. Within weeks Hosie was having five to eight convulsions per day. The vet opined that the seizures were a result of the residual damage to the dog's brain from the original snakebite; he recommended that Hosie be "put to sleep."

I brought Hosie home and contemplated the vet's advice. The procedure to end his life medically was expensive. I said to my wife, "Perhaps I should just take Hosie out in the woods as if we were going hunting. When he isn't looking I can mercifully and inexpensively end his life with one shot from my rifle." But even as I said it, I knew I could not do it. As I thought of training the sights of my rifle upon Hosie I knew there was no earthly way I could ever pull the trigger. I had to admit to my wife there was no way I could even drive the dog to the vet for execution. I asked her to find a student to take Hosie to the vet when I didn't know it was being done.

Two days later I came home from a lecture, and my wife told me gently, "It's over. Hosie's gone." I wept.

This episode in my life was about a dog. It was not an experience I had with my son. I could not even bring myself to kill a dog who was hopelessly ill. How radically different this was from Abraham's situation, yet my experience gave me a much greater appreciation of what Abraham was facing. God did not ask Abraham to kill his dog; God required that he kill his son, his only son, the son whom he loved.

For three days Abraham walked beside his son on the way to Mount Moriah. Isaac had no idea what was going on. The Scriptures say:

> Then on the third day Abraham lifted his eyes and saw the place afar off. And Abraham said to his young men, "Stay here with the donkey; the lad and I will go yonder and worship, and we will come back to you." (Gen. 22:4–5)

After three tortuous days of journey, Abraham and Isaac had still not arrived at their destination. Mount Moriah was visible but still was afar off. At this point Abraham ordered his servants to stop and wait with the donkey while he and his son continued on. He said they were going to the mountain to worship and that they would return. He said, "*We . . .* will come back." I can only speculate why Abraham said this. Was it an expression of undaunted faith that somehow God would rescind His command? Was it an attempt to conceal from his servants and from Isaac what his real mission was? I don't know, but I suspect he was crossing his fingers when he said it.

Far more heart-wrenching was the conversation that ensued between Abraham and his son:

> So Abraham took the wood of the burnt offering and laid it on

Isaac his son; and he took the fire in his hand, and a knife, and the two of them went together. But Isaac spoke to Abraham his father and said, "My father!"

And he said, "Here I am, my son."

Then he said, "Look, the fire and the wood, but where is the lamb for a burnt offering?"

And Abraham said, "My son, God will provide for Himself the lamb for a burnt offering." So the two of them went together. (Gen. 22:6–8)

Isaac noticed that something was missing. He saw that they had the wood and the fire necessary for a burnt offering, but the most important element was not present. Where was the lamb that would be slain? Who can imagine what went through Abraham's mind when Isaac asked the question? What could he say? "You are it! I am going to sacrifice *you.*" Hardly! Rather, Abraham answered in the Hebrew tongue with the words *"Jehovah-Jireh,"* which means "the Lord will provide."

This response by Abraham represents the first direct and explicit reference to divine providence found in the Bible. Again, we do not know if this utterance was an act of faith on Abraham's part, an expression of hope, or a thinly veiled attempt to disguise the expected outcome from Isaac. In any case, with this expressed promise of hope that God would provide a lamb for the sacrifice, the two of them continued their trek toward the mountain.

Finally the crucial moment arrived:

Then they came to the place of which God had told him. And Abraham built an altar there and placed the wood in order; and he bound Isaac his son and laid him on the altar, upon the wood. And Abraham stretched out his hand and took the knife to slay his son. (Gen. 22:9–10)

Surely the most difficult task Abraham ever performed in his life was the task of binding his son with ropes and placing him on the altar. By this time it had to have been absolutely clear to Isaac what was going on. Imagine the look in his eyes as he watched his father in stunned disbelief. Then Abraham raised the knife over his head, ready to plunge it into his son's heart. I'm sure he must have closed his eyes and trembled, the knife shaking out of control. And at the last possible second the voice of Jehovah-Jireh was heard from heaven:

> But the Angel of the LORD called to him from heaven and said, "Abraham, Abraham!"
> So he said, "Here I am."
> And He said, "Do not lay your hand on the lad, or do anything to him; for now I know that you fear God, since you have not withheld your son, your only son, from Me."
> Then Abraham lifted his eyes and looked, and there behind him was a ram caught in a thicket by its horns. So Abraham went and took the ram, and offered it up for a burnt offering instead of his son. And Abraham called the name of the place, The-LORD-Will-Provide; as it is said to this day, "In the Mount of the LORD it shall be provided." (Gen. 22:11–14)

Providence intervened. God called for Abraham to stop. A substitute was provided, a ram caught in the thicket, snared not by the thicket alone but by the very Creator of the thicket. Abraham passed the test of all tests and rested secure in the certainty of the fulfillment of God's promise for the future. Isaac would live and become the father of Jacob, who in turn would sire twelve sons whose progeny would be the nation of Israel.

Two thousand years later history noted the ultimate act of divine Providence. God would make the ultimate provision for human need. He provided another Lamb, a Lamb without blemish who was destined to die on a mountain named Calvary. Tradition locates that place as the exact same site as Old Testament Moriah. God took His Son, His only Son, the One whom He loved, Jesus, and placed Him on an altar on that mountain. And this time nobody hollered "Stop!"

Chapter 4

The Cry Heard 'Round the World

A BABY CRIED. THE WHIMPER THAT ESCAPED ITS LIPS changed the entire course of human history. All of Western civilization, all of Near Eastern history, indeed the entire course of human events was affected by this cry.

While the popular adage declares that "the devil is in the details," it is more accurate to avow that *God* is in the details. The doctrine of providence declares that God's providential rule extends to all things great and small, from the huge to the minute, the infinite to the infinitesimal.

Little things can have major consequences. We remember the proverb:

> For want of a nail, the shoe was lost;
> For want of the shoe, the horse was lost;
> For want of the horse, the rider was lost;
> For want of the rider, the battle was lost;
> For want of the battle, the kingdom was lost.
> And all from the want of a horseshoe nail.

Because of one solitary nail an entire kingdom was lost. It has also been said that a single grain of sand in the kidney of Oliver Cromwell changed the course of British and world history and that the beating of a butterfly's wings in China creates tiny perturbations in air currents that ultimately affect the weather on the opposite side of the earth. A small but fatal bullet ended the dream of an American Camelot. Little things can mean a lot.

What was the cry heard round the world? What infant whimper changed the destiny of Planet Earth? It was the cry of an infant cast adrift on the River Nile.

The children of Israel enjoyed privileged status in the land of Goshen, a small parcel of land in the ancient empire of Egypt. They had been granted this piece of real estate when Joseph reigned as prime minister of Egypt and invited his father and his brothers to settle in that place.

But things changed. As time passed a new king came to power who did not know Joseph. The memory of Joseph's promises had faded, and a new policy was enacted:

> Now there arose a new king over Egypt, who did not know Joseph. And he said to his people, "Look, the people of the children of Israel are more and mightier than we; come, let us deal shrewdly with them, lest they multiply, and it happen, in the event of war, that they also join our enemies and fight against us, and so go up out of the land." Therefore they set taskmasters over them to afflict them with their burdens. And they built for Pharaoh supply cities, Pithom and Raamses. But the more they afflicted them, the more they multiplied and grew. And they were in dread of the children of Israel. So the Egyptians made the children of Israel serve with rigor. And they made their lives bitter with hard bondage—in mortar, in brick, and in all manner of service in the field. All their service in which they made them serve was with rigor. (Exod. 1:8–14)

The descendants of Jacob were now prisoners in Egypt. They were enslaved and functioned as a slave-labor force. The pharaoh became ambivalent toward them. On the one hand he enjoyed the fruit of their labor as they toiled to build supply cities to protect the nation from possible future famines. (There is irony here as it was an earlier famine that caused the Israelites to migrate to Egypt in the first place.) On the other hand the pharaoh feared what every tyrant fears, an uprising by masses of people who revolt. To control the size and strength of the Jewish population, the new pharaoh issued a decree of limited genocide. He decreed the murder of every newborn Jewish male baby:

> Then the king of Egypt spoke to the Hebrew midwives, of whom the name of one was Shiphrah and the name of the other Puah; and he said, "When you do the duties of a midwife for the Hebrew women, and see them on the birthstools, if it is a son, then you shall kill him; but if it is a daughter, then she shall live." (Exod. 1:15–16)

The pharaoh was not content to command his soldiers to kill the Jewish babies. The task was assigned to Jewish midwives, who were commanded to carry out the slaughter of their own people. But in a heroic act of civil disobedience, the Hebrew midwives refused to carry out their task and tried to cover up their disobedience with lies (an interesting episode that is cited in the Christian ethics texts to show examples of justifiable acts of civil disobedience as well as extreme circumstances when the justifiable lie is uttered).

> But the midwives feared God, and did not do as the king of Egypt commanded them, but saved the male children alive.
> So the king of Egypt called for the midwives and said to them, "Why have you done this thing, and saved the male children alive?"
> And the midwives said to Pharaoh, "Because the Hebrew women are not like the Egyptian women; for they are lively and give birth before the midwives come to them."
> Therefore God dealt well with the midwives, and the people multiplied and grew very mighty. And so it was, because the midwives feared God, that He provided households for them.

So Pharaoh commanded all his people, saying, "Every son who is born you shall cast into the river, and every daughter you shall save alive." (Exod. 1:17–22)

It is interesting to note that the midwives found favor with God for their resistance to the decree of Pharaoh. They refused to do what God had forbidden. Further irony is seen in that the decree stipulated that the slain males were to be cast into the river. They were to be sunk in the Nile so as to never exercise any future threat to Pharaoh.

But one of the Hebrew women who bore a son took exceptional care to protect her son from the pharaoh's decree:

And a man of the house of Levi went and took as wife a daughter of Levi. So the woman conceived and bore a son. And when she saw that he was a beautiful child, she hid him three months. But when she could no longer hide him, she took an ark of bulrushes for him, daubed it with asphalt and pitch, put the child in it, and laid it in the reeds by the river's bank. And his sister stood afar off, to know what would be done to him. (Exod. 2:1–4)

With further irony, this Hebrew mother consigned her son's fate to the very river that was to be the place of disposal for dead infants. But she protected the baby from drowning by designing a crude vessel made watertight with asphalt and pitch lest leaks cause the ark to fill and sink. If ever a mother delivered her baby into the hands of the providence of God, it was this one! She set the ark afloat and let it be carried wherever the current would take it. As she set the little basket in the water, this mother had about as much reason to hope that her child would survive as Abraham did when he laid Isaac on the altar.

To this day one of the most vexing problems of science is the problem of predicting with accuracy the precise movements and flow of running water. Without warning, swirls and eddies develop that change the direction of flow. A basket floating in the Nile could

be affected by concealed rocks, floating branches, and even croco-
diles. Many mothers have abandoned their infants on the doorsteps
of hospitals, where there is a reasonable hope that they will be
found and cared for. But the only hope this mother had was in the
invisible hand of the God who made the river and ultimately governed its ebb and flow.

The child's oldest sister stood by the riverside, afar off, watching
the floating basket as it was carried along by the current. She was
exercising her own kind of providence, watching over the baby as
long as she could keep it in sight. At this moment the only eyes
upon the vessel were the eyes of the sister and the eyes of God.

Then a strange thing happened, something that some would
regard as a coincidence, a chance encounter, or a fortuitous event.
Someone else's eyes beheld the floating craft. What had attracted
these eyes to the river is a matter of conjecture. Perhaps it was a cry
from the infant:

> Then the daughter of Pharaoh came down to bathe at the river.
> And her maidens walked along the riverside; and when she saw the
> ark among the reeds, she sent her maid to get it. And when she
> opened it, she saw the child, and behold, the baby wept. So she had
> compassion on him, and said, "This is one of the Hebrews' chil-
> dren." (Exod. 2:5–6)

Of all the people on the face of the earth to spy the floating ark
at this place and at this time, it happened to be the pharaoh's
daughter. If this was a coincidence, it is one of the most remarkable
coincidences of all time. The Bible does not say she heard the baby
cry while it was being carried along the Nile. But when she had the
ark retrieved the baby was weeping, which makes me suspect it was
a cry that drew her attention to it in the first place. It may have
been a piercing yell or perhaps only a soft whimper. In any case the
child was discovered and evoked a sense of compassion from
Pharaoh's daughter.

Another irony also is in view here. This young woman's father has gone down in history as the prototypical example of a human being with a hardened heart. The refrain that runs through Exodus repeats the description of the hard heart of Pharaoh. But the heart of Pharaoh's daughter was soft. She had compassion upon crying babies, no matter their race. She exhibited a maternal instinct that led her to rescue the child.

It is significant that she recognized the baby was Hebrew. Obviously she was aware of her father's decree. She was risking her father's wrath, a princess defying the king, by stooping to aid the helpless Hebrew baby. Had she obeyed her father's decree she would have thrown the baby back into the river, and that would have been the end of it. There would be no "rest of the story." But this was not the end of it. Not by a long shot. It was not the end of it because the woman had compassion. The baby cried . . .

> Then [the baby's] sister said to Pharaoh's daughter, "Shall I go and call a nurse for you from the Hebrew women, that she may nurse the child for you?"
>
> And Pharaoh's daughter said to her, "Go." So the maiden went and called the child's mother. Then Pharaoh's daughter said to her, "Take this child away and nurse him for me, and I will give you your wages." So the woman took the child and nursed him. And the child grew, and she brought him to Pharaoh's daughter, and he became her son. So she called his name Moses, saying, "Because I drew him out of the water." (Exod. 2:7–10)

The events immediately following the discovery of the baby are almost as astonishing as the discovery itself. Obviously as she was standing afar off, the baby's sister saw his rescue from the river. But she could not be sure it was a rescue; it could have appeared to her as the ultimate disaster. Thinking quickly, she went to Pharaoh's daughter and volunteered to find a nurse for the baby. By this point she must have realized that Pharaoh's daughter had a tender heart and was not inclined to destroy the child.

Another irony may be seen in the vast difference caused by one letter in the princess's one-word response, the difference between an *n* and a *g*. When the sister volunteered to find a nurse, Pharaoh's daughter could have said, "No!" Instead she said, "Go"! So the sister went and called her mother, and the final irony took place. The baby's mother herself was hired to take care of the child. Her child was restored to her by the hand of Providence acting through the hand of Pharaoh's daughter.

Perhaps in reality this was not the final irony. Perhaps that occurred when the baby was named not by its mother but by the princess. (Though it is likely the mother had already named him.) The baby was named (or renamed) by Pharaoh's daughter, and it was this name by which he came to be known in history. Because he was drawn out of the water, the child was named Moses.

Moses was not merely rescued by the daughter of Pharaoh. Moses was given the advantage of being raised within the scope of Pharaoh's court. He was trained in the knowledge and skills of the Egyptian culture, which was crucial preparation for the tasks God would later assign to him. He was reared as a prince, with all the benefits accorded to that rank.

Playing "What If?"

It is at this point that we are tempted to indulge in playing the game of "What if?" What if Moses' mother had not successfully hidden him from Pharaoh's soldiers for three months? What if Moses' mother had not made the ark from reeds? What if the tiny craft had leaked and sunk to the bottom of the river? What if Pharaoh's daughter had not been at the riverside at the exact moment the ark floated by? What if she didn't have compassion? What if the baby hadn't cried?

The game of "What if?" involves contingencies, things that could conceivably occur—or not occur. They are dependent, "unnecessary" events. A necessary event is one that we believe could not have happened otherwise.

We are accustomed to think of fixed laws of nature that determine the sequence of certain events. We assume that when it rains the grass will become wet as a necessary consequence. We normally do not see this result as a pure contingency. Philosophically we do not know for sure that just because every time it rained in the past the grass got wet we can deduce absolutely that when it rains tomorrow the grass will get wet. We may say that the wetness of the grass tomorrow is a contingency. That is, it depends on whether it rains or if we water it with a hose or if dew forms in the morning. But we assume that if it does rain the grass will get wet as a necessary result. (The philosophical vagaries here were explored in great detail by the philosopher David Hume, who recognized that we do not have an immediate sensory apprehension of causal relationships but rather observe regular or customary relationships between events.)

The problem of contingencies relates to the broader question of causality, which we will explore more fully later. The question we are concerned with now is the relationship of contingencies to God. The issue is, Does anything happen contingently from His vantage point? We have said that God knows all contingencies but knows nothing contingently. At first glance this may seem like an arcane conundrum, an abstract consideration that is better left to philosophers. But it is important for us to think about it a bit as we seek a deeper understanding of the providence of God.

We remember that the term *providence* is derived from word forms that are at least somewhat concerned with foreknowledge. Foreknowledge belongs properly within the scope of God's omniscience. The omniscience of God is well attested in Scripture. We think, for example, of Psalm 139:

> O LORD, You have searched me and known me.
> You know my sitting down and my rising up;
> You understand my thought afar off.
> You comprehend my path and my lying down,
> And are acquainted with all my ways.
> For there is not a word on my tongue,

But behold, O LORD, You know it altogether.
You have hedged me behind and before,
And laid Your hand upon me.
Such knowledge is too wonderful for me;
It is high, I cannot attain it.

Where can I go from Your Spirit?
Or where can I flee from Your presence?
If I ascend into heaven, You are there;
If I make my bed in hell, behold, You are there.
If I take the wings of the morning,
And dwell in the uttermost parts of the sea,
Even there Your hand shall lead me,
And Your right hand shall hold me.
If I say, "Surely the darkness shall fall on me,"
Even the night shall be light about me;
Indeed, the darkness shall not hide from You,
But the night shines as the day;
The darkness and the light are both alike to You.

For You formed my inward parts;
You covered me in my mother's womb.
I will praise You, for I am fearfully and wonderfully made;
Marvelous are Your works,
And that my soul knows very well.
My frame was not hidden from You,
When I was made in secret,
And skillfully wrought in the lowest parts of the earth.
Your eyes saw my substance, being yet unformed.
And in Your book they all were written,
The days fashioned for me,
When as yet there were none of them.

How precious also are Your thoughts to me, O God!
How great is the sum of them!
If I should count them, they would be more in number
   than the sand;
When I awake, I am still with You. (Ps. 139:1–18)

The psalmist declares that we are perfectly and completely known by God. He knows what we are going to say before we say it. He has the capacity to know the end from the beginning. His knowledge extends down to the smallest details. He not only knows what we will say but He also knows everything we possibly could say. He knows all the possible contingencies. Yet there is nothing contingent about His knowledge; it does not depend upon what we will do. He doesn't have to wait to see which fork in the road we choose to know which fork we most certainly *will* choose. He knows the future precisely because He wills the future.

It was not a surprise to God that Pharaoh's daughter went to the riverside on a fateful day in human history. It was no surprise to Him that the baby cried. He ordained that the baby cry, and He ordained that it cry at the precise moment it cried. God did not leave all this to chance.

We play with the "what ifs?" and speculate on the course of history had the baby not cried. We could surmise that if the baby had not cried there would have been no Moses. Had there been no Moses there would have been no incident at the burning bush. No burning bush, no Exodus. No Exodus, no giving of the Law at Sinai. No Law, no prophets. No prophets, no Jesus. No Jesus, no cross. No cross, no redemption. No redemption, no Christianity. No Christianity, no Western civilization as we know it. All of this if a baby in a homemade ark had failed to cry at precisely the right moment.

But there is no "what if?" in God. He is a God whose providence is in the details.

Chapter 5

Everything Is Against Us?

ADAM SMITH REFERRED TO PROVIDENCE AS "THE INVISIBLE hand of God." Because God is invisible to us, we often fail to recognize His active presence in human affairs. Because we cannot peer into the transcendent realm, many things appear to happen by chance or as mere contingencies. We also have a tendency to misread the hand of God in history. This was surely the case in the life of the patriarch Jacob. Jacob had a life-changing experience at Bethel when he had an unexpected encounter with God:

> Now Jacob went out from Beersheba and went toward Haran. So he came to a certain place and stayed there all night, because the sun had set. And he took one of the stones of that place and put it at his head, and he lay down in that place to sleep. Then he dreamed, and behold, a ladder was set up on the earth, and its top reached to heaven; and there the angels of God were ascending and descending on it. (Gen. 28:10–12)

Jacob's midnight dream is the origin of the children's song "We Are Climbing Jacob's Ladder." The significance of the ladder was that it served as a link, a means of access, between heaven and earth. It is significant for us because we live in an age where God seems remote and unreachable. Modern humanity has an acute sense of the absence of God. There seems to be an unbridgeable chasm between the realm of nature and the realm of supernature, between the immanent and the transcendent. It is as if a chasm or an unscalable wall bars access to heaven. We use ladders to bridge the gap—scale the wall—between the earth and higher places.

Jacob's experience is the event later alluded to by Jesus when He declared to Nathaniel that he would see the angels ascending and descending upon the Son of Man. Jesus was the incarnation of Jacob's ladder, the One who in incarnation would make visible to us the invisible God.

When Jacob awoke from his dream he made an important observation. He said:

> "Surely the LORD is in this place, and I did not know it." And he was afraid and said, "How awesome is this place! This is none other than the house of God, and this is the gate of heaven!"
>
> Then Jacob rose early in the morning, and took the stone that he had put at his head, set it up as a pillar, and poured oil on top of it. And he called the name of that place Bethel; but the name of that city had been Luz previously. (Gen. 28:16–19)

What a poignant scene: Jacob was suddenly aware that God had been present—but he had missed it. He exclaimed that the place was awesome, made so by the presence of God. This incident had to be formative to Jacob's personal understanding of God. From this point on, Jacob should have been able to trust in the promises of God because in the vision at Bethel God had said to him, "Behold, I am with you and will keep you wherever you go, and will bring you back to this land; for I will not leave you until I have done what I have spoken to you" (Gen. 28:15).

God promised He would keep Jacob wherever he went. He promised to bring him back to the land and solemnly declared that

He would not leave him. From that day forward Jacob had these promises to rely upon. He did not have a continuous vision of the presence of God; he had the promise but not the sight. If God was going to remain with Jacob He would do it in an invisible manner. Jacob would not be able to see the presence of God.

If we fast-forward the story of Jacob's life we will see that his confidence in the promise of God obviously faded. Jacob began to trust more in what he saw than in what he could not see; he began to trust in outward appearances. This is nowhere clearer than when Jacob had to deal with the loss of his son Joseph and the consequences of that event.

Years later a severe famine struck the land of Egypt and all the neighboring nations, including Canaan, and Jacob instructed his sons to cross the border and go down to Egypt to seek provisions there. Egypt alone had resources sufficient to meet the crisis of the famine. When the sons of Jacob came to the royal court in Egypt they met with the prime minister—their brother Joseph whom they did not recognize. In the years since they had sold their brother he had changed. He was dressed in the garb of a royal official and spoke to them through an interpreter. Joseph recognized his brothers and understood every word they were saying among themselves, but they did not recognize him. Joseph accused his brothers of being spies. They denied the charge and said:

> "Your servants are twelve brothers, the sons of one man in the land of Canaan; and in fact, the youngest is with our father today, and one is no more."
>
> But Joseph said to them, "It is as I spoke to you, saying, 'You are spies!' In this manner you shall be tested: By the life of Pharaoh, you shall not leave this place unless your youngest brother comes here. Send one of you, and let him bring your brother; and you shall be kept in prison, that your words may be tested to see whether there is any truth in you; or else, by the life of Pharaoh, surely you are spies!" So he put them all together in prison three days. (Gen. 42:13–17)

Joseph knew the youngest brother who had been left at home was Benjamin. He longed to hear news of his father, Jacob, and he longed to see Benjamin again. So he contrived this test for his brothers. Then, after three days, Joseph proposed a different plan:

"Do this and live, for I fear God: If you are honest men, let one of your brothers be confined to your prison house; but you, go and carry grain for the famine of your houses. And bring your youngest brother to me; so your words will be verified, and you shall not die."

And they did so. (Gen. 42:18–20)

This plan caused great consternation among the brothers. Suddenly their treachery of years earlier against Joseph came to their minds and assaulted their consciences. They said to one another :

"We are truly guilty concerning our brother, for we saw the anguish of his soul when he pleaded with us, and we would not hear; therefore this distress has come upon us."

And Reuben answered them, saying, "Did I not speak to you, saying, 'Do not sin against the boy'; and you would not listen? Therefore behold, his blood is now required of us." But they did not know that Joseph understood them, for he spoke to them through an interpreter. And he turned himself away from them and wept. Then he returned to them again, and talked with them. And he took Simeon from them and bound him before their eyes. (Gen. 42:21–24)

Reuben, the eldest brother, assumed that the present calamity that befell his brothers and him was a result of their guilt. He was trying to read the invisible hand of Providence. He was correct in assuming that God was involved with their predicament. He was also correct in assuming that their present state was intimately connected to their past sinful action. What he did not recognize was that this "judgment" that was falling upon them was profoundly mixed with grace. Reuben saw the judgment but missed the grace. His apprehension of the purpose of God's providence was incomplete. The rest of the story had not yet been written, and Reuben had no clue to how things would work out or what God was doing in this moment.

Gradually Joseph's plan began to take shape. He planted incriminating evidence in the sacks the brothers had brought to carry grain back to Canaan:

> Then Joseph gave a command to fill their sacks with grain, to restore every man's money to his sack, and to give them provisions for the journey. Thus he did for them. So they loaded their donkeys with the grain and departed from there. But as one of them opened his sack to give his donkey feed at the encampment, he saw his money; and there it was, in the mouth of his sack. So he said to his brothers, "My money has been restored, and there it is, in my sack!" Then their hearts failed them and they were afraid, saying to one another, "What is this that God has done to us?" (Gen. 42:25–28)

Now, instead of holding all the brothers hostage except one, Joseph reversed his tactic and sent all the brothers home except one. He kept Simeon back as a single hostage. When the brothers opened their grain sacks they found the money Joseph had had planted there. They were terrified, knowing that now they could not prove their innocence and that the Egyptian official would probably have Simeon killed.

Reading that they cried out, "What is this that God has done to us?" we again note that these men had some notion of Providence, but their assumptions were all wrong. They knew they had not stolen the money. But the incriminating evidence was there. Who had put it there? They did not know whose human hand had placed the contraband there, but they did understand by whose ultimate hand it had come to be placed there. They discerned the invisible hand of God in all this as much as they missed the purpose of it.

The brothers returned to Jacob and related to him all that had happened. Jacob's reaction was one of great fear and unbridled grief:

> Then it happened as they emptied their sacks, that surprisingly each man's bundle of money was in his sack; and when they and their father saw the bundles of money, they were afraid. And Jacob their father said to them, "You have bereaved me: Joseph is no more, Simeon is no more, and you want to take Benjamin. All these things are against me."
>
> Then Reuben spoke to his father, saying, "Kill my two sons if I do not bring him back to you; put him in my hands, and I will bring him back to you."
>
> But he said, "My son shall not go down with you, for his brother is dead, and he is left alone. If any calamity should befall him along the way in which you go, then you would bring down my gray hair with sorrow to the grave." (Gen. 42:35–38)

Jacob poured out his heart in grief, articulating the reason for his bereavement. He said, "Joseph is no more, Simeon is no more. All these things are against me." But Jacob was jumping to erroneous conclusions. Were these conclusions reasonable? By all means. He had every reason to assume that Joseph was no more; he had empirical evidence to back up that inference. Perhaps he had saved the bloody robe his sons had brought home when they told him Joseph had been killed by a wild animal. And he obviously remembered his sons' earlier testimony:

> So they took Joseph's tunic, killed a kid of the goats, and dipped the tunic in the blood. Then they sent the tunic of many colors, and they brought it to their father and said, "We have found this. Do you know whether it is your son's tunic or not?"
>
> And he recognized it and said, "It is my son's tunic. A wild beast has devoured him. Without doubt Joseph is torn to pieces." Then Jacob tore his clothes, put sackcloth on his waist, and mourned for his son many days. And all his sons and all his daughters arose to

comfort him; but he refused to be comforted, and he said, "For I shall go down into the grave to my son in mourning." Thus his father wept for him. (Gen. 37:31–35)

Jacob had every reason to believe that Joseph was dead. He had the eyewitness testimony, not merely from strangers, but from his own sons. The brothers all corroborated the story of Joseph's death. In addition, he had the blood evidence on the coat. He did not have the advantage of modern techniques of serology or of DNA testing that would have shown that the blood on the coat was not Joseph's blood. In reality Jacob was a victim of a conspiracy. He was grief-stricken when the brothers reported Joseph's death to him. He went into deep mourning, tearing his clothes to pieces and donning sack-cloth. His sons and his daughters arose to comfort him. We assume that the attempts of comfort made by his daughters were genuine. We assume they were not part of the conspiracy and were also in mourning for their brother. But the comfort of the brothers was one of unmitigated hypocrisy. They knew very well that it was not Joseph's blood on the garment.

The conspiracy went on for years as the brothers continued to live a lie with their own father. They saw his grief. They watched his mourning. For years every reference to Joseph necessitated the continuation of the lie and the cover-up. The whole episode could be called Josephgate. At any rate, Jacob was convinced that Joseph was dead.

The Two Levels of Knowledge

The famous philosopher Immanuel Kant, in his epic work *The Critique of Pure Reason*, argued that we seek knowledge at two distinct levels or in two distinct realms. He distinguished between the *phenomenal realm* and the *noumenal realm*. The phenomenal realm refers to that level of reality we perceive with our five senses, the realm we can see, hear, feel, smell, or taste. It is the realm of empirical experience, the realm investigated by the natural sciences.

The noumenal realm, Kant declared, is the realm of God, the self, and of metaphysical essences (things in themselves). He argued that neither naked reason nor empirical investigation can penetrate the noumenal realm. We cannot move from the phenomenal realm to the noumenal realm by rational or empirical investigation. Kant was agnostic about our ability to know anything about God, the self, or about essences. He believed our knowledge is limited to the realm of phenomena. For Kant the realm of Providence is the realm of speculation or of practical reason. We may have to live "as if" there were a God, for practical reasons, but we can have no real knowledge of God or of His providence.

Certainly Jacob was making his conclusions on the basis of phenomenal experience. Again these conclusions have to be seen as reasonable, given the evidence Jacob had to work with. He was walking by sight, not by faith. In this particular case the evidence drawn from the phenomena he had at his disposal was misleading. His conclusion was wrong. In reality Joseph was not "no more." Joseph was "some more." He was alive and well and reigning as the prime minister of Egypt.

Jacob was convinced that Simeon also was dead—and again he was wrong. This was the second time Jacob's sons had returned home to him with one of their brothers missing. He had every reason to suspect that the same fate that had befallen Joseph had now befallen Simeon. Yet, humanly speaking, Simeon had never been safer in his life than he was at that moment. He was in the custody of his brother Joseph. Indeed, it was a protective custody. Simeon had nothing to fear from Joseph. But neither Jacob nor Simeon was aware of that reality.

So Jacob came to his ultimate conclusion. In light of the disappearance of Joseph and now Simeon, Jacob declared, "All these things are against me."

*

All Things Work Together for Good

Jacob's lament sounds very much like the cry we have all made at some point in our lives. We remember the pitiful little ditty: "Nobody loves me; everybody hates me; I'm going to go eat worms." Jacob was ready for a diet of worms. He was convinced that everything was working against him, but nothing could have been further from the truth! The reality was that everything was working *for* him. God in His providence was working all things together for good for Jacob and his descendants. But all the outward signs pointed to the very opposite.

One of the axiomatic slogans of the Christian faith is the Latin phrase *deus pro nobis,* which means "God for us." In the New Testament the apostle Paul exclaimed: "If God is for us, who can be against us?" (Rom. 8:31). That God is for us is the cardinal point of the doctrine of providence. God was for Jacob. He had promised that to Jacob years before the brothers returned to him from Egypt without Simeon. But Jacob could not see how this could be. The very moment when he was most sure that all things, including God, were working against him, all things by the hand of God were actually working for him. God had sent Joseph into Egypt for a purpose. That purpose would be worked out on every page of redemptive history.

After Jacob's lament, Judah, the third eldest son, later persuaded him to allow the brothers to return to Egypt to get grain and try to recover Simeon. Judah pledged his own life as a safeguard for Benjamin, saying, "Send the lad with me, and we will arise and go, that we may live and not die, both we and you and also our little ones. I myself will be surety for him; from my hand you shall require him. If I do not bring him back to you and set him before you, then let me bear the blame forever" (Gen. 43:8–9).

Jacob was finally persuaded by Judah's entreaty and pledge. He relented in resignation and said, "Take double money in your hand, and take back in your hand the money that was returned in the mouth of your sacks; perhaps it was an oversight. Take your brother also, and arise, go back to the man. And may God Almighty give you mercy before the man, that he may release your other brother and Benjamin. If I am bereaved, I am bereaved!" (Gen. 43:12–14)

Jacob was ready to take one more step of faith. He acknowledged the possibility that it could end in disaster. He risked the further loss of his beloved Benjamin. This time he did not regret his decision. The brothers went back to Egypt, secured the grain, obtained the release of Simeon, and discovered the identity of Joseph. When they returned home with both Simeon and Benjamin and news of the well-being of Joseph we are told that "the spirit of Jacob their father revived" (Gen. 45:27). Then Jacob declared: "It is enough. Joseph my son is still alive. I will go and see him before I die" (Gen. 45:28).

In the final analysis, the providence of God was enough for Jacob. It should also be enough for us. Jacob lived to see something of the hidden hand of God. He did not see all of the purpose of providence unfold before his eyes, but he saw enough.

[Chapter 6]

Providence and Government

I ONCE HAD THE OPPORTUNITY TO MEET WITH A MEMBER of the United States Senate. During a discussion over lunch at the Senate dining room in the Capitol the conversation focused on the government's involvement in warfare and the conscription of citizens via the draft. The Senator leaned toward pacifism. As we debated the classical just-war theory, the senator made a remark that left me stunned. He said, "I do not believe the government ever has the right to force its citizens to do anything." I responded by saying, "Then it would seem that you are saying the government does not have the right to govern."

My reply was met by a blank stare. Finally the senator asked me what I meant. I explained that government involves a legal form of force; we might even define government itself as "legalized force." When the government enacts laws, those laws are not passed on to the citizens as mere suggestions. They are requirements that are backed up with a form of coercion. Every law that is passed restricts somebody's freedom. With the law always comes law enforcement, and law enforcement carries the weight of coercion. If I refuse to obey the laws, the law enforcement agencies have the authority to force my compliance by a multitude of methods.

The Political Dimension of God's Providence

The providence of God also has a political dimension to it, touching the arena of politics in at least two significant ways. In the first place God's providence has reference to His government of the universe. Insofar as God reigns and rules over His creation, He exercises a kind of cosmic political authority. Although Jesus said to Pontius Pilate that His kingdom was not *of* this world, that did not mean that His kingship was not *over* this world. In His ascension Christ was enthroned in heaven as King of the kings and Lord of the lords. Christ has the highest "political" office in the cosmos. All earthly magistrates are under His dominion and are answerable to Him for how they exercise their authority.

One of the most central motifs of Scripture is the recurring theme of the kingdom of God. A kingdom is a realm ruled by a monarch. God is the Super Monarch of the cosmos. He not only governs the realm of nature by His natural laws, He also governs the world of human affairs. He steers the courses of the stars and the flight of the birds as they migrate. He governs the course of human history. He causes kingdoms and empires to rise and makes kingdoms and empires fall. No king is ever elevated to the throne apart from the providence of God.

The Bible makes it clear that government is a human institution that is ordained and instituted by God. As Paul declared:

> Let every soul be subject to the governing authorities. For there is no authority except from God, and the authorities that exist are appointed by God. Therefore whoever resists the authority resists the ordinance of God, and those who resist will bring judgment on themselves. For rulers are not a terror to good works, but to evil. Do you want to be unafraid of the authority? Do what is good, and you will have praise from the same. For he is God's minister to you for good. But if you do evil, be afraid; for he does not bear the sword in vain; for he is God's minister, an avenger to execute wrath on him who practices evil. (Rom. 13:1–4)

In this passage Paul avers that "the authorities that exist" (or the powers that be) are appointed by God; they function as God's ministers. I once was asked to address a breakfast gathering during the inauguration of the governor of Florida. In that address I stated that the inauguration was in many respects similar to the ordination, or installation, of a pastor. Both the pastor and the governor serve in roles of ministry. One ministers to the church; the other ministers to the state. The church and the state are two different institutions with two different roles to perform. It is not the task of the church to be the state; nor is it the task of the state to do the work of the church. But both institutions are ordained by God, and both institutions are to be "under" God.

In the eighteenth century the concept of separation of church and state meant one thing; today it is understood in radically different terms. Originally the concept pointed to a clear division of labor between two institutions and guarded the borders between the two. Today a not-so-subtle shift has occurred, and now the idea of separation of church and state has come to mean the separation of state and God. The state wishes to be autonomous, not answerable or accountable to God. In a word, the government has declared its independence from God.

This is nothing new in history. In the Middle Ages monarchs sanctioned their rule by appealing to the theory of the divine right of kings. Usually coronation was done by the church. In England the monarch was and still is given the title *Defensor Fide* or "Defender of the Faith." But there were few kings who voluntarily submitted to the authority of God. Even in theocratic Israel it was the kings who, more often than not, were leaders in godlessness.

The common resistance of earthly rulers to the reign of God over them may be seen in the sentiments of Psalm 2:

> Why do the nations rage,
> And the people plot a vain thing?
> The kings of the earth set themselves,
> And the rulers take counsel together,

Against the LORD and against His Anointed, saying,
"Let us break Their bonds in pieces
And cast away Their cords from us."

He who sits in the heavens shall laugh;
The LORD shall hold them in derision.
Then He shall speak to them in His wrath,
And distress them in His deep displeasure:
"Yet I have set My King
On My holy hill of Zion."

"I will declare the decree:
The LORD has said to Me,
'You are My Son,
Today I have begotten You.
Ask of Me, and I will give You
The nations for Your inheritance,
And the ends of the earth for Your possession.
You shall break them with a rod of iron;
You shall dash them to pieces like a potter's vessel.'"

Now therefore, be wise, O kings;
Be instructed, you judges of the earth.
Serve the LORD with fear,
And rejoice with trembling. (Ps. 2:1–11)

The psalm reflects a conspiracy among the kings of this world. They hold a summit meeting in which they declare their independence from God. They hold a joint council of war and aim the sum of their military might toward heaven. The response of God is holy laughter. The arsenal of human weapons is viewed as mere popguns by the Almighty.

God's derisive laughter quickly turns to wrath as He warns against the rejection of His rule and that of His anointed. He rebukes the kings for their folly, warning them that He will break them with a rod of iron. They are called to rule, not with the arrogance of pretended autonomy, but with fear and trembling. The fear and trembling are to be motivated by an awareness that their authority is a delegated authority. It is extrinsic, not intrinsic. All authority on heaven and earth has been given by the Father to the Son. Every lesser authority is subject to Him.

In one sense we say that America is not a theocracy. It differs in its legal structure and framework from Old Testament Israel. Our government is secular in nature. But this is only a matter of degree. All human government is theocratic in the sense that God is the ultimate ruler over all. Our political leaders may not be theocratically organized at the human level, but in terms of Providence they are all inescapably theocratic.

The government of God is part of His work of upholding, or sustaining, His creation. The first visible form of earthly government was manifested at the entrance to the Garden of Eden:

> Then the LORD God said, "Behold, the man has become like one of Us, to know good and evil. And now, lest he put out his hand and take also of the tree of life, and eat, and live forever"—therefore the LORD God sent him out of the garden of Eden to till the ground from which he was taken. So He drove out the man; and He placed cherubim at the east of the garden of Eden, and a flaming sword which turned every way, to guard the way to the tree of life. (Gen. 3:22–24)

The flaming sword of the angelic sentinel posted at the east gate of Eden was the first weapon of law enforcement to appear on the earth.

Theologians have argued over the origin and purpose of earthly government. Augustine argued that earthly government was not so much a necessary evil as a necessity of evil. That is, it was sin's entrance into the world that made earthly government necessary. Government is invoked to settle disputes between sinners, to ensure just weights and measures in an environment where people are inclined to cheat, and to oversee the keeping of contracts where parties are given to lie and to break promises. Government is designed to be an instrument of justice that protects the innocent from crimes like theft and murder. The preservation, maintenance, and protection of life is a major responsibility for government. None of these things would require such oversight if human beings were not sinful.

Aquinas opined that, even without sin, government would still be necessary to manage the division of labor that would be in effect even in an unfallen society. However, both Aquinas and Augustine agreed that the real presence of evil makes human government necessary. The magisterial Reformers of the sixteenth century agreed with this analysis. They recognized that governments can become corrupt in the extreme but that even wicked government is better than no government. Society cannot long endure in the context of anarchy.

The angel with the flaming sword who guarded the gate of Eden indicated the presence of government. Access was restricted, and the flaming sword was the instrument of coercion given to enforce the law. In Romans 13 Paul speaks of the "power of the sword" that is given to civil magistrates. That power is given by God. It is the right to enforce law. Indeed, it is more than a right; it is a duty delegated to the authorities.

It is interesting that government officials are often called "the authorities." This title calls attention to the fact that they have authority. They have been "authorized" to bear the sword.

The power of the sword carries with it more than the authority to rattle it. The state is given the right to use the sword. This principle lies behind the authorization God gives to human government to execute criminals in capital crimes and to wage war in a just cause. The sword is given to curb evildoers and to promote justice. If a peaceful country is invaded by a lawless aggressor, the civil magistrate has the responsibility to defend the country's borders from attack. These matters may become exceedingly complex, as international law and international conflicts reveal.

In his analysis of warfare Thomas Aquinas argued that all wars are evil but not everyone's involvement in war is evil. There can be situations when use of the sword is justified. Again, this view rests on the premise that it is God who delegates the use of the sword to earthly rulers.

History makes it clear that there are manifold times when earthly governments abuse the power and authority they have been given by God. The sword has been used to shed innocent blood; it has been used for wars of conquest and for tyrannical oppression. When this occurs the earthly government should fear the sword of the Lord. God will judge the nation and its use of the sword. The book of Revelation gives dreadful warnings on this point:

> Then another angel came out of the temple which is in heaven, he also having a sharp sickle.
>
> And another angel came out from the altar, who had power over fire, and he cried with a loud cry to him who had the sharp sickle, saying, "Thrust in your sharp sickle and gather the clusters of the vine of the earth, for her grapes are fully ripe." So the angel thrust his sickle into the earth and gathered the vine of the earth, and threw it into the great winepress of the wrath of God. And the winepress was trampled outside the city, and blood came out of the winepress, up to the horses' bridles, for one thousand six hundred furlongs. (Rev. 14:17–20)

In the beginning of The Revelation Jesus is depicted as having a sword coming out of His mouth. The prophecy of the book warns of the judgment that is to come via the sword of the Lord. In Revelation 14 the instrument of judgment is a sharp sickle, a kind of sword. The passage quoted above is the biblical text upon which the famous song "The Battle Hymn of the Republic" is based. The lyrics "Mine eyes have seen the glory of the coming of the Lord" were incorporated into the battle song for the Union army in the War Between the States. It was based upon the assumption that God was on the side of the North in the Civil War. That sentiment was not shared by the people of the South. Men like Lee and

Jackson were convinced that God favored the South because they believed that the cause of states' rights was the cause of God.

Determining Which Side God Is On

How do we determine if God is on "our side" in a dispute? There are several ways to go about this determination. One thing we can do is look at the outcome of the conflict. Stonewall Jackson used to lead his soldiers in prayer before battle and say to them, "The battle is ours; the outcome is God's." Jackson was surely correct in his assumption that the outcome was God's. He understood that Providence would govern the results. Yet even if one side in a conflict wins the battle or even the war, this, in itself, is no guarantee that God is on the side of the victor. As we will see later, there are times within the providence of God that the purpose of God is that the "right side" loses.

The other way of determining whose side God is on is by the careful application of biblical principles of ethics. God is ultimately always on the side of righteousness. He takes no delight in the ways of wickedness. Though for a season the wicked may prosper and the righteous may suffer, at the final bar of divine justice it is the wicked who will not prosper and the righteous who will receive their reward. Injustice is real. It occurs every day. Indeed, it is the present reality of injustice that will be rectified in the final judgment.

We remember the agnosticism of Immanuel Kant, who argued that the invisible realm of God cannot be known on the basis of reason or empirical investigation. Yet even Kant argued for the existence of God on the grounds of "practical reason." His argument flowed out of a concern for justice and ethics. He approached the issue transcendentally by asking the question, "What is necessary for ethics to be meaningful?" He argued for his famous categorical imperative, his version of the Golden Rule. He saw this as a practical necessity for society to survive and surely would have agreed with Dostoevsky's maxim that "if there is no God, all things are permissible."

For Kant, ethics would be both meaningless and undesirable if there were no ultimate justice. Why should someone be righteous if in the final analysis crime really does pay? Since justice does not always prevail in this world, Kant argued for the practical necessity of life after death and, more importantly, for judgment after death so that the scales of justice might finally be balanced. It was the obverse of this that Nietzsche argued when in his nihilism he declared that God is dead and there is no meaning to human existence. Ethics becomes a matter of preference for the strong.

Kant's practical argument was really an argument, not from providence, but for providence. It was an appeal for an ultimate Judge who would serve as an ultimate Governor. There are too many cases of injustice in this world to base our ultimate trust in justice on human courts. All too often Lady Justice's blindfold slips, and she peeks. Jesus alluded to this in His parable of the unjust judge:

> Then He spoke a parable to them, that men always ought to pray and not lose heart, saying: "There was in a certain city a judge who did not fear God nor regard man. Now there was a widow in that city; and she came to him, saying, 'Get justice for me from my adversary.' And he would not for a while; but afterward he said within himself, 'Though I do not fear God nor regard man, yet because this widow troubles me I will avenge her, lest by her continual coming she weary me.'"
>
> Then the Lord said, "Hear what the unjust judge said. And shall God not avenge His own elect who cry out day and night to Him, though He bears long with them? I tell you that He will avenge them speedily. Nevertheless, when the Son of Man comes, will He really find faith on the earth?" (Luke 18:1–8)

The promise of Christ is that God will exercise justice. He will vindicate and avenge His people wherever they have suffered injustice in this world. In this parable though true justice is delayed it is not denied; it will surely come. It is a call to trust in the providence of God. The parable ends on a note that sounds abrupt. It ends with a question regarding faith and its presence at the time of the return of Christ.

We may wonder why Christ ended the parable the way He did. He seems to anticipate that His people would struggle with the problem of delayed justice, and He called for a faith that would endure periods of human injustice, confident of divine providence.

It may be difficult for us to view the providence of God in political terms because we are accustomed to making a radical distinction between politics and God. But theology is intensely political in the sense that it bridges the gap between earthly government and divine government. Politics is about government; it is an arena that is intensely important to us because it is where we live out our daily lives. We are interested in politics because what happens in that arena has a direct impact upon us.

We are living in an age in America with unprecedented intrusion of federal and state government in our lives. For example, the last time I looked there were twenty-eight different taxes imposed on the commercial production and sale of a loaf of bread. We can hardly take two paces without bumping into government. The government intrudes on the highway and on the sidewalk. It seems ubiquitous. Government touches so much of our lives that we have to ask where God is in all this. We know He is not a registered Republican or a registered Democrat. His government transcends all political parties. God is not a registered voter in human affairs. Yet He is the One who casts the deciding ballot in every human election. It is only by and through His providence that anyone ever wins or loses an election.

Chapter 7

The Visible Hand

WE HAVE SEEN THAT THE GOVERNMENT OF DIVINE PROVIDENCE extends to the smallest things. It involves the micromanagement of the details. But God's providential government also extends to the great things of history, to the rise and fall of nations, kings, and governments. In this regard God's providence extends to the macromanagement of the universe and of world history.

We have seen that it is a dangerous thing to make rash assumptions that God is always on our side. It is true that, because we are the people of God, God is always *Deus pro nobis*, always for us, but this being "for us" must always be seen in an ultimate sense. In the proximate, or more immediate, sense there are times when God is against us. Thus the paradox is seen that even when God is against us He is for us. As a father chastens the child he loves, so God at times will thwart our plans and work against us precisely because He is working for our own ultimate good.

The Rise and Fall of Evil Empires

When we assume that God is always on the side of our nation, we make this assumption at our own peril. This assumption, which is usually made more from the vantage point of jingoism, or chauvinism, than from a sound theology, rests on at least two other assumptions. The first is that ours is a Christian or godly nation, or that our nation always acts in a godly manner.

When Ronald Reagan was president of the United States he once referred to the former Soviet Union as the "evil empire." I do not dispute that assessment. The atrocities committed during the regime of Joseph Stalin are a matter of record. But what about America? Could not our own nation at times warrant the epithet "evil empire"? It is sheer arrogance to assume that our nation always acts in a righteous manner and is always in the right. The issue is not so much, Is God on our side? but, Are we on the side of God?

The second, equally dangerous assumption is that God always sides in His immediate providence with the most righteous nation in a dispute. The Bible is replete with the record of God's using more wicked nations to chastise less wicked nations for the purposes of His providential rule. This was the situation that burdened the prophet Habakkuk:

> O LORD, how long shall I cry,
> And You will not hear?
> Even cry out to You,
>   "Violence!"
> And You will not save.
> Why do You show me iniquity,
> And cause me to see trouble?
> For plundering and violence are before me;
> There is strife, and contention arises.
> Therefore the law is powerless,
> And justice never goes forth.
> For the wicked surround the righteous;
> Therefore perverse judgment proceeds. (Hab. 1:1–4)

Habakkuk was a patriot. He loved his own nation and was distressed with the circumstances of its historical situation. Israel was being oppressed by a foreign enemy, and Habakkuk complained that God was not hearing his pleas and was refusing to save His people in the midst of violence. Later he continued his protest:

> Are You not from everlasting,
> O LORD my God, my Holy One?
> We shall not die.
> O LORD, You have appointed them for judgment;
> O Rock, You have marked them for correction.
> You are of purer eyes than to behold evil,
> And cannot look on wickedness.
> Why do You look on those who deal treacherously,
> And hold Your tongue when the wicked devours
> A person more righteous than he? (Hab. 1:12–13)

Habakkuk was having difficulty reconciling God's holy nature with His seemingly unholy providence. He complained that God was too holy to even gaze upon wickedness, yet He seemed to be over-looking the obvious evil of the enemy. Habakkuk raised the supreme question that arises from every study of the providence of God: "Why do you look on those who deal treacherously, and hold Your tongue when the wicked devours a person more righteous than he?"

His complaint was that God seemed to be favoring the wicked (or at least the more wicked) over the righteous. The bottom line of Habakkuk's protest was that God was not fair. Habakkuk removed himself to his watchtower to await the answer of God. He was determined to hear God speak in His own divine vindication, even though God had spoken earlier in terms that should have silenced Habakkuk:

> "Look among the nations and watch—
> Be utterly astounded!
> For I will work a work in your days
> Which you would not believe, though it were told you.
> For indeed I am raising up the Chaldeans,

A bitter and hasty nation
Which marches through the breadth of the earth,
To possess dwelling places that are not theirs.
They are terrible and dreadful;
Their judgment and their dignity proceed from themselves.
Their horses also are swifter than leopards,
And more fierce than evening wolves.
Their chargers charge ahead;
Their cavalry comes from afar;
They fly as the eagle that hastens to eat. (Hab. 1:5–8)

Here God acknowledges that He is using a wicked nation (the Chaldeans) for His own purposes. This is not the first time in Jewish history that God used evil empires as rods to chasten His own people. If we look back to the book of Judges, we see a refrain that is frequently repeated:

> Then the children of Israel did evil in the sight of the LORD, and served the Baals; and they forsook the LORD God of their fathers, who had brought them out of the land of Egypt; and they followed other gods from among the gods of the people who were all around them, and they bowed down to them; and they provoked the LORD to anger. They forsook the LORD and served Baal and the Ashtoreths. And the anger of the LORD was hot against Israel. So He delivered them into the hands of plunderers who despoiled them; and He sold them into the hands of their enemies all around, so that they could no longer stand before their enemies. Wherever they went out, the hand of the LORD was against them for calamity, as the LORD had said, and as the LORD had sworn to them. And they were greatly distressed.
>
> Nevertheless, the LORD raised up judges who delivered them out of the hand of those who plundered them. (Judg. 2:11–16)

This is the oft-repeated refrain: that Israel did what was evil in the sight of the Lord. A pattern emerged: When the people of Israel did evil, God would raise up one of their enemies to chasten them and subject them to bondage. Then the people would repent and cry out for deliverance, and every time God would then raise up a judge to deliver His people. When the people were delivered they would rejoice. But in short order they would once again do what was evil in the sight of the Lord. As the pattern was repeated the point became clear that God would not hesitate to use a more wicked nation to punish Israel when Israel fell into disobedience.

This is the point Habakkuk should have known. God may empower a wicked nation for his own use for a season, but it is always *for a season*. These wicked nations always get their just reward in the end. The great kingdoms of world history have all become corrupt. They have all fallen in due time, a time that is in the hands of Providence. Eventually Habakkuk came to understand the words of his own book: "The LORD is in His holy temple. Let all the earth keep silence before Him" (Hab. 2:20).

When God revealed Himself to Habakkuk, the prophet was reduced to terror:

> When I heard, my body trembled;
> My lips quivered at the voice;
> Rottenness entered my bones;
> And I trembled in myself,
> That I might rest in the day of trouble.
> When he comes up to the people,
> He will invade them with his troops.
>
> Though the fig tree may not blossom,
> Nor fruit be on the vines;
> Though the labor of the olive may fail,
> And the fields yield no food;
> Though the flock may be cut off from the fold,
> And there be no herd in the stalls—
> Yet I will rejoice in the LORD,
> I will joy in the God of my salvation.

The LORD God is my strength;
He will make my feet like deer's feet,
And He will make me walk on my high hills.

To the Chief Musician. With my stringed instruments.
(Hab. 3:16–19)

While Habakkuk was voicing his complaint, God was in His holy temple. The earth was not keeping silent before Him. Habakkuk was not keeping silent before Him. When God manifested Himself to the prophet he was reduced to quaking in terror. Out of his terror, however, came a renewed confidence in God's providence. He learned the cardinal point of faith, that whatever comes to pass, no matter how calamitous it may appear in the moment, there is reason for joy and confidence. The person who puts his trust in Providence acquires feet like those of a deer, able to walk securely in high and dangerous places.

The Fall of Babylon

That God reigns over macro forces is perhaps most clearly seen in Daniel's record of the fall of Belshazzar, king of Babylon. The story of Belshazzar's feast includes an incident in history in which the invisible hand of God became visible in a literal sense:

Belshazzar the king made a great feast for a thousand of his lords, and drank wine in the presence of the thousand. While he tasted the wine, Belshazzar gave the command to bring the gold and silver vessels which his father Nebuchadnezzar had taken from the temple which had been in Jerusalem, that the king and his lords, his wives, and his concubines might drink from them. Then they brought the gold vessels that had been taken from the temple of the house of God which had been in Jerusalem; and the king and his lords, his wives, and his concubines drank from them. They drank wine, and praised the gods of gold and silver, bronze and iron, wood and stone. (Dan. 5:1–4)

The ancient city of Babylon was one of the wonders of the world. It was considered an impregnable fortress. Surrounded by extraordinarily high and thick walls, it seemed invulnerable to attack. The wealth of the city was great enough to withstand protracted sieges from enemy nations. Secular history is divided on the question of how the city was defeated and who the king was who is named by Daniel as Belshazzar.

The historians Xenophon, Herodotus, and Josephus agree that the Persians conquered Babylon during a riotous festival being hosted by Babylonian royalty. They say the Persians gained access to the city by damming the river Euphrates, allowing the soldiers to enter the city by a huge drain pipe under the wall. The troops could not knock down the city walls or scale them. Instead they found a way to go under them. That Belshazzar was hosting a great feast at the time indicated the sense of security he had.

It was not unusual for prominent Oriental monarchs to host huge parties with as many as a thousand guests; the large crowds were a sign of the monarchs' opulence and power. It was the custom at such events for the king to be seated on an elevated rostrum at a separate table so he could observe his guests and be seen plainly by them. On this occasion Belshazzar commanded that the sacred vessels of the Jews be brought to the banquet hall to be used for the drinking of wine. To the Jewish people this would have been a profound insult and to the God of Israel an unmitigated act of blasphemy. It also indicated the supreme arrogance of Belshazzar.

In all probability drinking the wine was not a mere incident of riotous partying but was an act of pagan religion in which the pagan deities were praised, or "toasted," by the assembly. This only served to exacerbate the insult to God. It echoed the earlier taunting of the God of Israel committed by the Philistines during the period of the Judges, when the ark of the covenant was captured and placed as a trophy in the temple of Dagon. During the party the arrogance of Belshazzar was interrupted by an astonishing event:

In the same hour the fingers of a man's hand appeared and wrote opposite the lampstand on the plaster of the wall of the king's palace; and the king saw the part of the hand that wrote. Then the king's countenance changed, and his thoughts troubled him, so that the joints of his hips were loosened and his knees knocked against each other. (Dan. 5:5–6)

Belshazzar's composure was destroyed at the sight that unfolded before his eyes. The king did not see the entire hand that was writing but only the fingers, a sight that jolted him awake from his drunken stupor. He obviously sensed that he was viewing a preternatural phenomenon.

As the writing appeared clearly on the wall that had been plastered with lime, the king's countenance changed instantly. His face turned ashen, and he was stricken in his conscience. The record says his knees knocked together in uncontrolled terror. The reference to the loosening of his joints indicated that his hips were no longer firm enough to support the weight of his body.

In his terror, Belshazzar summoned various classes of Babylonian wise men to interpret the writing that haunted him:

The king cried aloud to bring in the astrologers, the Chaldeans, and the soothsayers. The king spoke, saying to the wise men of Babylon, "Whoever reads this writing, and tells me its interpretation, shall be clothed with purple and have a chain of gold around his neck; and he shall be the third ruler in the kingdom." Now all the king's wise men came, but they could not read the writing, or make known to the king its interpretation. Then King Belshazzar was greatly troubled, his countenance was changed, and his lords were astonished. (Dan. 5:7–9)

It is significant that all three groups of wise men called to the banquet site to interpret the words on the wall were pagans. There was no immediate call for Daniel or any other leaders from the Jewish people. It was only after the pagan wise men failed to interpret the writing that Daniel was summoned. The king had offered an extravagant reward to the person who could read the message, indicating the depth of his desperation. He promised the purple cloth, the golden chain, and a third of the kingdom. These accouterments were all symbols of high rank in the ancient world.

It was the queen who suggested that Daniel be called to interpret the words on the wall. In all probability this was the queen-mother, not the wife of Belshazzar (since the king's wives were noted as being present at the feast). If this was Nebuchadnezzar's widow, she would have ample knowledge of Daniel's prophetic and interpretative gifts. In response to her suggestion, Daniel was summoned:

> Then Daniel was brought in before the king. The king spoke, and said to Daniel, "Are you that Daniel who is one of the captives from Judah, whom my father the king brought from Judah? I have heard of you, that the Spirit of God is in you, and that light and understanding and excellent wisdom are found in you. Now the wise men, the astrologers, have been brought in before me, that they should read this writing and make known to me its interpretation, but they could not give the interpretation of the thing. And I have heard of you, that you can give interpretations and explain enigmas. Now if you can read the writing and make known to me its interpretation, you shall be clothed with purple and have a chain of gold around your neck, and shall be the third ruler in the kingdom." (Dan. 5:13–16)

Daniel was not impressed with the flattering words spoken to him by Belshazzar. He declined the king's offer of reward and reminded Belshazzar of the encounter his father had had with God:

> "O king, the Most High God gave Nebuchadnezzar your father a kingdom and majesty, glory and honor. And because of the majesty that He gave him, all peoples, nations, and languages trembled and feared before him. Whomever he wished, he executed; whomever he wished, he kept alive; whomever he wished, he set up; and whomever he wished, he put down. But when his heart was lifted

up, and his spirit was hardened in pride, he was deposed from his kingly throne, and they took his glory from him. Then he was driven from the sons of men, his heart was made like the beasts, and his dwelling was with the wild donkeys. They fed him with grass like oxen, and his body was wet with the dew of heaven, till he knew that the Most High God rules in the kingdom of men, and appoints over it whomever He chooses." (Dan. 5:18–21)

The final comment of this record displays Daniel's warning to Belshazzar that even the king of Babylon is subject to the transcendent rule of Providence. God rules the kingdom of men and appoints whom He wills to rule. Then Daniel spoke God's words of indictment over Belshazzar before he proceeded to interpret the handwriting on the wall:

"But you his son, Belshazzar, have not humbled your heart, although you knew all this. And you have lifted yourself up against the Lord of heaven. They have brought the vessels of His house before you, and you and your lords, your wives and your concubines, have drunk wine from them. And you have praised the gods of silver and gold, bronze and iron, wood and stone, which do not see or hear or know; and the God who holds your breath in His hand and owns all your ways, you have not glorified. Then the fingers of the hand were sent from Him, and this writing was written." (Dan. 5:22–24)

Daniel explained that the inscribed message had come from the hand of God. The words were indeed a divine indictment. The reason given was that "the God who holds your breath in His hand and owns all your ways, you have not glorified." These words anticipate the words used by Saint Paul at the Areopagus in Athens when he rebuked the pagan philosophers for their superstition. When he beheld their altar "TO THE UNKNOWN GOD" Paul chided them for their ignorance, saying it was in God that they lived and moved and had their being (see Acts 17:16–32). Likewise, Daniel reminded Belshazzar that the very breath of his life was held in the same hand that wrote on the wall.

We might wonder about the severity of this indictment. After all, Belshazzar was not a Jew. How could he be expected to know about the God of Israel? The answer is that he was culpable on two counts. In the first place God has revealed His true character to all people (including Belshazzar and including you and me) in creation. As Paul teaches in Romans 1, this general revelation is so clear that no philosopher or king—in Belshazzar's day or in ours—has any excuse to ignore it. In the second place, Belshazzar had the special knowledge of God that had been made manifest to his own family; Belshazzar could not claim ignorance as an excuse. With these words Daniel then proceeded to interpret the mysterious message:

"And this is the inscription that was written:

MENE, MENE, TEKEL, UPHARSIN.
This is the interpretation of each word. MENE: God has numbered your kingdom, and finished it; TEKEL: You have been weighed in the balances, and found wanting; PERES: Your kingdom has been divided, and given to the Medes and Persians." Then Belshazzar gave the command, and they clothed Daniel with purple and put a chain of gold around his neck, and made a proclamation concerning him that he should be the third ruler in the kingdom. (Dan. 5:25–29)

Belshazzar had been weighed in the balance and had been found wanting on the divine scales; he was too light. He was deficient in moral worth. His kingdom was to be dissolved. The glory of Babylon was about to end. She would be conquered by another nation. The text then declares that on "that very night, Belshazzar, king of the Chaldeans, was slain."

From this incident in biblical history the expression "the handwriting is on the wall" was born. It survives to this day as an expression that harbinges ruin and the certainty of impending defeat or judgment. In Belshazzar's case, the handwriting on the wall demonstrated the futility of victory when the *invisible* hand of Providence became *visible* in His hand of judgment.

[*Chapter 8*]

The Mystery of Providence and Concurrence

ONE OF THE QUESTIONS I AM FREQUENTLY ASKED IS, "What is the meaning of Ligonier?" The question is asked because I work for a ministry called Ligonier Ministries. The assumption that often lurks behind the question is that *Ligonier* is an esoteric Greek word that has some spiritual or religious meaning. The assumption is incorrect. I usually answer the question with the cryptic reply, "*Ligonier* is the reason why you speak English rather than French."

Here is the story: The name Ligonier refers to a small village in western Pennsylvania with a population of about two thousand people. It was there, in the Ligonier Valley, that our ministry was founded; when we moved to Orlando we simply retained the name. In the middle of the eighteenth century, the village of Ligonier had a population of ten thousand people—all British soldiers under the command of General Forbes (for whom Forbes Field, the predecessor to Three Rivers Stadium, was named). These soldiers were amassed at Fort Ligonier in preparation for an assault against Fort Duquesne, a place of strategic importance during the French and Indian War. At that time, the French controlled the inland territory of the new world, including the inland waterways, with fortresses in Montreal in the north, New Orleans in the south, and Fort

Duquesne in between. British expansion westward from New England and Virginia was blocked by this French territorial control.

When the "Great Commoner" William Pitt was prime minister of England, he ordered General Braddock to launch an attack of Fort Duquesne. Braddock's troops marched from Virginia westward through the Cumberland Gap toward the fort in what is now western Pennsylvania. It was almost an impossible mission because moving the heavy artillery and supply wagons over the mountains was so difficult. To make matters worse, the French came out to meet the British en route, and the British suffered a bloody defeat. General Braddock was killed in the battle. One of Braddock's lieutenants had five horses shot out from under him. A bullet passed through the back of this lieutenant's shirt without even scratching his skin. Amazingly, the lieutenant lived to tell about it. His name was George Washington. Just one more instance of a small detail that changed the course of history!

After this crushing defeat, William Pitt ordered General Forbes to plan another assault on Fort Duquesne. This time Lieutenant Washington made use of his surveying skills to map a different route over the difficult terrain. Ten small forts were built along the way to serve as supply depots. The last fort from which the attack would be launched was named Fort Ligonier in honor of Lord Ligonier, an expatriated Frenchman who served on the cabinet of William Pitt's administration. (Another detail of history is that the slave-trade ship that carried Kunte Kinte of *Roots* fame from Africa to America was *The Lord Ligonier*.)

During the French and Indian War, nine of the ten forts built for this assault were captured by the enemy. The only one that survived was Fort Ligonier. (To this day the battle of Fort Ligonier is reenacted every autumn during Fort Ligonier Days.)

When the British moved out against the French from Fort Ligonier, the French sneaked in behind them and burned Fort Ligonier to the ground—and then fled from the British. The British rebuilt the fort and named it after the prime minister, calling it Fort Pitt. It was later renamed Pittsburgh, the city known as the

"Gateway to the West" long before St. Louis claimed the title. Once the British controlled this territory, the inland waterways were opened for westward expansion. River traffic could now begin in Pittsburgh and proceed down the Ohio River to the Mississippi and all the way to New Orleans.

I grew up in what is now modern Pittsburgh. During my childhood there was no threat of Indian attacks; that was considered ancient history. Yet in elementary school we made field trips to the center of downtown Pittsburgh to an area called "The Point," where the famous "confluence" of the Allegheny and Monongahela Rivers form the great Ohio River.

It is ironic that the confluence of events that changed the course of American history involved a geographical site of crucial confluence.

The Doctrine of Confluence

The term *confluence* refers to the "flowing together" of two or more currents. It derives from the Latin root that means to flow "with." The term *confluence* can also be rendered from its synonym, *concurrence.* Ideas or events concur when they agree with one another or flow together at the same time. This word *confluence* is crucial for our understanding of the doctrine of the providence of God because an aspect of the doctrine of providence is the doctrine of concurrence, or confluence.

The doctrine of concurrence refers to historical events in which the work of Providence has been acted out through human agencies. That means at the same time human agents are acting, God is acting in and through them. We remember the assertion of the Westminster Confession of Faith, which says:

God, from all eternity, did, by the most wise and holy counsel of his own will, freely, and unchangeably ordain whatsoever comes to pass: yet so, as thereby neither is God the author of sin, nor is violence offered to the will of the creatures; nor is the liberty or contingency of second causes taken away, but rather established.

Some very important concepts are contained in this section of the Confession. The first is the reference to what is called the "biblical apriori," the axiom that God is not the author of sin. This means that God neither commits sin Himself, nor does He work in such a manner that He coerces His creatures to sin. At the same time the Confession avows that God ordains whatsoever comes to pass. He ordains the actions of human beings but not in such a way that He does violence to the will of His creatures or nullifies second causes.

The Most Vexing Mystery

Here we run head-on into what remains as perhaps the most vexing mystery of Christian faith. The mystery focuses on the interconnection between the providential work of the Creator and the real work of His creatures. Before we attempt to tackle this great problem, we must first make an important distinction—the distinction between a mystery and a contradiction. In almost every theological book I have written I have found it necessary to explain this distinction. I do not grow weary of repetition at this point because this distinction is so critical to Christian thought. (If it is a woman's prerogative to change her mind, so the chief prerogative of the theologian is to make distinctions!)

A contradiction is easy to define. Indeed, it is defined by the classic rules of logic. The law of non-contradiction says that A cannot be both A and non-A at the same time and in the same relationship. That is, something cannot be what it is and not be what it is at the same time and in the same sense. I can be a father and a son at one and the same time but not in the same sense or in the same relationship. A tree can be a plant and a source of shade at the same time. But it cannot be a tree and not be a tree at the same time and in the same sense.

To say that God is sovereign and that man is free is not a contradiction in terms. To say that God is sovereign and that man is autonomous would be a contradiction. If God is sovereign, man cannot be autonomous (a law unto himself). If man is autonomous, God could not be sovereign. These two concepts are mutually exclusive; they cancel out one another. To have a sovereign God coexisting with an autonomous creature would be like having the coexistence of an irresistible object and an immovable object.

Let's consider for a moment the idea of an immovable object coexisting with another object that exerts an irresistible force. We then contemplate the classic question: "What happens when an irresistible force meets an immovable object?"

We can't have a stand-off. If the immovable object moves, then it can no longer be deemed immovable. If it doesn't move, then the irresistible force is not irresistible. There is no other alternative.

It is important to note that the idea of an immovable object, considered in itself, is a rationally possible concept. Likewise, the idea of an immovable object is a rationally possible concept. What is rationally impossible is the idea of both of these things existing at the same time.

So it is with the ideas of divine sovereignty and human autonomy. Each concept when considered alone is a rationally possible idea. The concept of divine sovereignty is not self-contradictory. Likewise, the idea of human autonomy is not self-contradictory. What is self-contradictory is the idea of the mutual existence of the two. If one of them is true, the other cannot possibly be true.

So far this exercise in rational possibility is easy. The difficulty arises when we change the terms a bit. The term *autonomy* means absolute freedom. Something, such as God, can be both sovereign and autonomous. That is, it is possible for a being to be both absolutely free and absolutely sovereign. The two characteristics can coexist in one being. We have seen, however, that the two qualities cannot coexist in *two beings*.

It is important to see that we can have a concept of freedom that falls short of autonomy. That is, we can conceive of a being that has freedom within limits. The real problem emerges when we try to square the relationship between divine sovereignty and human freedom. It seems then that the attribute of sovereignty belongs necessarily to God. If God is not sovereign, He is not God. It also seems that freedom belongs necessarily to the idea of a moral agent. If man is to be deemed responsible for his actions, he must have some degree of freedom. That freedom need not be absolute; it need not be autonomous. If the creature has some freedom, however limited, then the creature is responsible to whatever degree it is free.

The concepts of divine sovereignty and limited human freedom are not mutually exclusive. We know from Scripture that man is not sovereign. I have heard it said that man's freedom limits God's sovereignty. If that were so then man, not God, would be sovereign. It is not that human freedom limits God's sovereignty. God's sovereignty is absolute and unlimited. Rather, it is God's sovereignty that limits human freedom. God's sovereignty transcends human freedom and rules over it. We are free only to the degree that God allows that freedom.

Though these distinctions give some relief to the vexing problem of the relationship between God's providence and human actions, they do not solve the problem altogether. We are still left with the problem of how man can be free at all in light of God's providence. If God ordains or wills everything that comes to pass, we wonder how that affects human volitional actions.

One way this is frequently answered is by an appeal to God's permissive will. The distinction is made between God's "decretive will," by which He sovereignly brings to pass whatever He decrees, and His "permissive will" that leaves room for the moral actions of His creatures. However, this solution often oversimplifies the question. If God is omnipotent, then He clearly has the power to prevent any event from happening that actually happens. If I choose to sin this afternoon, God has the *power* to prevent me from sinning if He so chooses. He also has the *right* to prevent me from sinning since He is sovereign. If he "permits" my sin, this does not mean He sanctions it or gives His permission in the sense that He deems it lawful. He may let it occur without intervening to stop it. This is what is meant by His permissive will. He lets it happen. But what God permits to happen He still *chooses* to permit. That is, since He could stop it and decides not to stop it, He exercises His permission according to His good pleasure. In some sense He ordains that it happens or else it could not happen.

We can push this reasoning, not only to the moral actions of creatures themselves, but to the desires in the human heart that produce such actions. The human desire for sin is also under God's sovereign control. I cannot even desire to sin unless God in His providence "permits" it, and He will not permit it unless it accords with His ultimate will. In a word, I cannot even sin unless it is ordained in some sense by God. We will explore this more fully later, but for the moment we will merely observe it in passing. The key phrase here is the one used by Augustine when he argued that God, *in some sense*, ordains everything that comes to pass. The qualifying phrase "in some sense" was Augustine's attempt to preserve the mystery of the relationship between divine sovereignty and human responsibility.

That we meet mystery here is inescapable. We have seen that it is impossible for contradictory forces to be at work ultimately but not for mysterious things to be at work. There is a big difference between a mystery and a contradiction. The two are not the same thing, even though they may have certain things in common with each other. The big point of commonality between a mystery and a contradiction is our failure to understand either of them. A mystery may be defined as something that is true that we do not understand. Notice I did not say that a mystery is something we *cannot* understand. There are many examples in history wherein previous mysteries have been solved. To say that a present mystery is unsolvable presumes that we have reached the zenith of knowledge, indeed omniscience.

One of the fundamental axioms of theology is the incomprehensibility of God. The Latin phrase *finitum non capax infinitum* applies; it means "the finite cannot grasp the infinite." Even in heaven there will be some elements of God we will not be able to comprehend. Even in our glorified state we will still be finite. We will still be creatures. The Bible gives ample reason to believe that in heaven we will understand far more things than we presently grasp, but even then there will be limits to our knowledge.

As we have seen, the point of contact between mystery and contradiction is that we do not understand either. A contradiction is inherently unintelligible. It is not understood because it *cannot* be understood. One frequent and fatal refuge from this problem is the assertion that God is able to understand contradictions. If this were true it would be fatal to Christianity. If real contradictions can be resolved in the mind of God, then it would mean that anything God has ever spoken or revealed is now suspect. If contradictions that are false to us can be true to God, then we would have no way of knowing if the very opposite of what God reveals as truth is actually true. If God can hold to contradictions, then perhaps in His mind there is no difference between Christ and Antichrist, between obedience and disobedience, between good and evil.

Rather than groveling in the murky madness of dialectical theology, in which both poles of a contradiction are affirmed, let us be clear in our assertion that not even God can understand a real contradiction. Even God cannot be God and not be God at the same time and in the same relationship. There is much room in the Christian faith for paradox and mystery, but no room for contradictions. God may understand all mysteries and all paradoxes, but He understands no contradictions.

Because mystery and contradiction have the lack of our understanding of them in common, many feel no tension with confusing them and are quite willing to affirm the presence of contradiction in Christian truth. This flight into the absurd makes God both irrational and a liar and makes the Holy Spirit the Author of confusion. Nor is it proper to call a bona fide contradiction merely a mystery. Contradiction falsifies truth claims; mysteries do not. Again, because we cannot understand how God can be sovereign and man be autonomous at the same time, we dare not affirm them both as a "mystery." These propositions, if held at the same time, are more than a mystery; they are a contradiction. At least one of them must be false.

The church has been careful in her historical confessions to flee from contradictory assertions. I once heard a philosophy professor ridicule Christianity because of the doctrine of the Trinity. He said that Christianity is absurd because it asserts a blatant contradiction in this doctrine. The professor should have known better than to make that charge. To say that God is one in essence and three in person is not a contradiction. It violates no rule of reason. Indeed, the test of Venn diagrams—a system of logic that uses circles to represent sets and their relationships—can be applied to prove the doctrine of the Trinity is not contradictory. Indeed, if the church declared that God was one in essence and three in essence or one in person and three in person at the same time and in the same sense, then the formulation *would* be contradictory and thus falsified. The church does not say that. It does not declare that God is one in A and three in A. Rather it says that He is One in A and three in B. Now, how a being can be One in essence and three in person is beyond our present understanding. It remains a profound mystery to us. But it is not a contradiction.

I have labored this point because the integrity of the biblical faith is at stake. In our age of irrationality even professing Christians get caught up in this confusion and do violence to Christian truth claims. The doctrine of God's providence, particularly as it concerns concurrence or confluence, is replete with mysteries. If these mysteries resolve into contradictions, then something has to go. We hope it will not be the nature or character of God that will be negotiated.

In our day it is precisely the nature of God Himself that is under attack. This attack comes not only from skeptics but from the lips and pens of professed evangelicals. With the corruption of our fundamental understanding of the nature and character of God comes always and everywhere the corruption of the doctrine of divine

Providence in its wake. In our zeal to protect the dignity of man and the ground of his moral responsibility (both of which are noble and necessary concerns), we must jealously guard against so weakening our understanding of God that His very essence and character are denuded.

Chapter 9

Joseph's Technicolor Coat: A Profile of Concurrence

THE DOCTRINE OF CONCURRENCE MAY BE SEEN IN A manifold number of cases in sacred Scripture. We see it, for example, in the work of Judas, whose treachery resulted in the betrayal and subsequent execution of Christ. His evil deed was a fulfillment of prophecy as he became the human instrument through whom Jesus was delivered to the Gentiles for judgment. Though Caiaphas, Herod, and Pontius Pilate all had roles in this, the greatest drama of human history, it is Judas who shoulders the lion's share of the blame.

Can Judas stand at the last judgment and demand a reward for his contribution to the Atonement? Cannot he say, "Without me Good Friday would be Bad Friday"? That we mark the anniversary of the death of Christ by the designation "Good" Friday reveals that we view the events of that day, as diabolical as they were in their human inception, as the most salutary day in human history. Had Judas attempted to claim virtue for his heinous crime because God used it for redemption, he would most surely have failed in the attempt. Though God, in His saving providence, wrought ultimate good out of this act, this does not exonerate Judas from his crime.

The same could be said for Pharaoh. Without the hardened heart of Pharaoh there would have been no Exodus. Could the Egyptian monarch then claim a reward in heaven for his contribution to the Exodus? To ask the question is to answer it.

Grand Schemes of Concurrence

Could the Chaldeans who stole Job's livestock at the instigation of Satan claim credit for Job's passing of his supreme trial? The story of Job is a drama with a large cast of characters. The cast includes Job, the Sabeans, the Chaldeans, Satan, and God. Who was it that afflicted Job? Was it God? Satan? The Chaldeans? It was all of them together in a grand scheme of concurrence.

Let us consider the culpability of the Chaldeans. Can we not hear them at the bar of God's justice blaming Satan for their attack against Job? "The devil made us do it" is their plea. Attention then turns to the devil, who pleads, "God made me do it." This type of buck-passing was first heard in the Garden of Eden when Adam blamed Eve for his transgression and Eve blamed the serpent. The serpent had no one left to blame except God.

In reality Satan did not coerce the Chaldeans to steal Job's livestock. It was not as if the Chaldeans were pristine, pure, moral virgins who were suddenly forced against their wills to steal from Job. They were cattle rustlers from the beginning. God had put a hedge around Job, protecting him from the assaults of men and of Satan. When the hedge was removed Satan seized the opportunity to unleash his assault against Job. He made use of the wicked desires of the Chaldeans, who had undoubtedly coveted Job's livestock all along. God's purpose in Job's trial was to vindicate Job against the slander of Satan and to demonstrate His own power and glory. Satan's purpose was to mock God and prove that when left to themselves men will serve Satan rather than God. The Chaldeans had their own agenda. They weren't interested in the cosmic drama that left Job vulnerable to them in the first place. They were interested in the cattle and their own commercial profit. We have here multiple players with various motives, all working together to accomplish the will of God. This coworking, or synergism, is an example of the mystery of concurrence.

Perhaps the clearest example of concurrence in Scripture is found in the narrative history of Joseph. Joseph's problems began in his youth when he was but seventeen years old. Because he was the child of Jacob's old age, the patriarch showed favoritism toward Joseph. This provoked profound jealousy and anger among Joseph's brothers. Their hatred toward him was exasperated by Joseph's relating to them of his mysterious dreams:

> Now Israel loved Joseph more than all his children, because he was the son of his old age. Also he made him a tunic of many colors. But when his brothers saw that their father loved him more than all his brothers, they hated him and could not speak peaceably to him.
>
> Now Joseph had a dream, and he told it to his brothers; and they hated him even more. So he said to them, "Please hear this dream which I have dreamed: There we were, binding sheaves in the field. Then behold, my sheaf arose and also stood upright; and indeed your sheaves stood all around and bowed down to my sheaf."
>
> And his brothers said to him, "Shall you indeed reign over us? Or shall you indeed have dominion over us?" So they hated him even more for his dreams and for his words.
>
> Then he dreamed still another dream and told it to his brothers, and said, "Look, I have dreamed another dream. And this time, the sun, the moon, and the eleven stars bowed down to me."
>
> So he told it to his father and his brothers; and his father rebuked him and said to him, "What is this dream that you have dreamed? Shall your mother and I and your brothers indeed come to bow down to the earth before you?" And his brothers envied him, but his father kept the matter in mind. (Gen. 37:3–13)

While Jacob was annoyed by the matter of Joseph's dreams, the brothers were more than annoyed. They began to plot his removal from their midst:

Now when they saw him afar off, even before he came near them, they conspired against him to kill him. Then they said to one another, "Look, this dreamer is coming! Come therefore, let us now kill him and cast him into some pit; and we shall say, 'Some wild beast has devoured him.' We shall see what will become of his dreams!"

But Reuben heard it, and he delivered him out of their hands, and said, "Let us not kill him." And Reuben said to them, "Shed no blood, but cast him into this pit which is in the wilderness, and do not lay a hand on him"—that he might deliver him out of their hands, and bring him back to his father. (Gen. 37:18–22)

When the discussion led to plans of murder, Reuben intervened to suggest an alternative plan. He advised them not to kill Joseph outright but to leave him stranded in a pit. Reuben planned to secretly return to the pit and rescue Joseph. But this plan was scrapped when another alternative presented itself with the passing of a caravan headed for Egypt:

So it came to pass, when Joseph had come to his brothers, that they stripped Joseph of his tunic, the tunic of many colors that was on him. Then they took him and cast him into a pit. And the pit was empty; there was no water in it.

And they sat down to eat a meal. Then they lifted their eyes and looked, and there was a company of Ishmaelites, coming from Gilead with their camels, bearing spices, balm, and myrrh, on their way to carry them down to Egypt. So Judah said to his brothers, "What profit is there if we kill our brother and conceal his blood? Come and let us sell him to the Ishmaelites, and let not our hand be upon him, for he is our brother and our flesh." And his brothers listened. Then Midianite traders passed by; so the brothers pulled Joseph up and lifted him out of the pit, and sold him to the Ishmaelites for twenty shekels of silver. And they took Joseph to Egypt. (Gen. 37:23–28)

Judah was the third-eldest brother; Reuben was the eldest, the brother destined to receive the patriarchal blessing and the promise of the kingdom. Yet Reuben schemed with his brothers to not only get rid of Joseph but to gain a profit from doing so.

The events that followed in Joseph's life resemble a shortened version of Alexander Dumas's *The Count of Monte Cristo*. First Joseph was sold as a slave to Potiphar, a high-ranking official in the Egyptian government. But in exile and in slavery Joseph did well, gaining the praise of his master for the excellent service he rendered to him. Then Joseph was falsely accused by Potiphar's wife when he spurned her sexual advances. The scorned woman demanded vengeance against Joseph, and Joseph was thrown into prison and held there for years. He was in a foreign country, removed from the culture where the God of his fathers was worshiped, isolated from everything that was precious to him. We can't help but wonder how he was able to maintain the integrity of his faith in those lost years. But he did. It was his faith that had led him to resist the illicit invitations of Potiphar's wife:

So it was, from the time that he had made him overseer of his house and all that he had, that the Lord blessed the Egyptian's house for Joseph's sake; and the blessing of the Lord was on all that he had in the house and in the field. Thus he left all that he had in Joseph's hand, and he did not know what he had except for the bread which he ate.

Now Joseph was handsome in form and appearance.

And it came to pass after these things that his master's wife cast longing eyes on Joseph, and she said, "Lie with me."

But he refused and said to his master's wife, "Look, my master does not know what is with me in the house, and he has committed all that he has to my hand. There is no one greater in this house than I, nor has he kept back anything from me but you, because you are his wife. How then can I do this great wickedness, and sin against God?" (Gen. 39:5–9)

One of the characteristics of the Old Testament is that it portrays the heroes of the faith with warts and all. Many of these heroes are described in terms similar to Shakespearean heroes who display fatal moral blemishes. But we need a microscope to find any such flaw in Joseph. He appears in almost Christlike virtue throughout the narrative of his life. When he refused the advances of Potiphar's wife, he said he could not sin against his master, Potiphar, and violate the trust he had received from him. Beyond that he realized that to acquiesce to her desires would mean that he would have to sin against God. He was unwilling to do that. Because of his obedience to God, Joseph ended up in prison. There he made friends with his fellow prisoners:

> Then Joseph's master took him and put him into the prison, a place where the king's prisoners were confined. And he was there in the prison. But the LORD was with Joseph and showed him mercy, and He gave him favor in the sight of the keeper of the prison. And the keeper of the prison committed to Joseph's hand all the prisoners who were in the prison; whatever they did there, it was his doing. The keeper of the prison did not look into anything that was under Joseph's authority, because the LORD was with him; and whatever he did, the LORD made it prosper. (Gen. 39:20–23)

Even in prison Joseph excelled. He was a model prisoner and earned the respect of his jailer. The salient point of his incarceration was that while he was in captivity God was with him and sustained him by His tender mercy. Joseph had been abandoned by his brothers and abandoned by Potiphar, but he was not abandoned by God.

The friends Joseph made in prison also let him down:

> And they said to him, "We each have had a dream, and there is no interpreter of it."
> So Joseph said to them, "Do not interpretations belong to God? Tell them to me, please."
> Then the chief butler told his dream to Joseph, and said to him, "Behold, in my dream a vine was before me, and in the vine were

three branches; it was as though it budded, its blossoms shot forth, and its clusters brought forth ripe grapes. Then Pharaoh's cup was in my hand; and I took the grapes and pressed them into Pharaoh's cup, and placed the cup in Pharaoh's hand."

And Joseph said to him, "This is the interpretation of it: The three branches are three days. Now within three days Pharaoh will lift up your head and restore you to your place, and you will put Pharaoh's cup in his hand according to the former manner, when you were his butler. But remember me when it is well with you, and please show kindness to me; make mention of me to Pharaoh, and get me out of this house. For indeed I was stolen away from the land of the Hebrews; and also I have done nothing here that they should put me into the dungeon." (Gen. 40:8–15)

After Joseph interpreted the dreams of the butler and the baker, the butler was restored to the service of Pharaoh. But he forgot about Joseph. Joseph was left to languish in prison. It was not until a long time elapsed before Pharaoh himself was disturbed by a troubling dream that none of his wise men were able to interpret. Finally the butler remembered Joseph and commended his skills to Pharaoh.

When Joseph successfully interpreted Pharaoh's dream, he was rewarded by being elevated to the second-highest position in the land. All of this transpired to set the stage for Joseph's later reunion with his brothers. When the drama reached its climax and Joseph's true identity was revealed to his brothers, they cowered in terror, fearing Joseph's revenge:

When Joseph's brothers saw that their father was dead, they said, "Perhaps Joseph will hate us, and may actually repay us for all the evil which we did to him." So they sent messengers to Joseph, saying, "Before your father died he commanded, saying, 'Thus you shall say to Joseph: "I beg you, please forgive the trespass of your brothers and their sin; for they did evil to you."' Now, please, forgive the trespass of the servants of the God of your father." And Joseph wept when they spoke to him.

Then his brothers also went and fell down before his face, and they said, "Behold, we are your servants."

Joseph said to them, "Do not be afraid, for am I in the place of God? But as for you, you meant evil against me; but God meant it for good, in order to bring it about as it is this day, to save many people alive. (Gen. 50:15–20)

God's Higher Purpose in Mysteries of Concurrence

Joseph forgave his brothers according to the wishes of his father. He did not minimize their guilt but called attention to the higher purpose of God in the matter. He said, "You meant evil against me, but God meant it for good, in order to bring it about as it is this day, to save many people alive." This is the *locus classicus,* the very heart, of the biblical doctrine of concurrence. God in His providence was involved in the whole life of Joseph. It was by His hand that Joseph was brought into Egypt. This did not exonerate the brothers from their wicked actions, but God worked through the evil machinations of men in order to accomplish His purpose.

Joseph stressed the difference in the *intent* of God and of his brothers. The concept of intentionality lies at the heart of human personality and volition. Voluntary actions involve intent. The action of my beating heart is *in*voluntary; though I want my heart to beat, it does not beat because I intend it to. In contrast, moral actions are actions done for a reason, by intent. They are actions that are meant to be done. Indeed, we have provisions in the law for culpability in the case of "accidents." That culpability stretches as far as our intent. Perhaps we did not plan to smash our car into somebody else's, but we did mean to drive as fast as we were driving. If we hit another car while we are speeding, we are responsible for our negligence.

God's intentions are always good. There is no shadow of turning in Him, no lapses into negligence. He clearly intended for Joseph to be sold into slavery; His purpose in this was altogether holy. The means He used to accomplish this end were the wicked wills of His creatures. They intended something altogether different from God's intent. They meant evil. They committed evil. They were responsible for that evil.

We have seen already how the cry of a baby changed the course of history. Just as God exercised His providential care of the infant Moses, so He governed all things that occurred in the life of Joseph. If we play the "what if?" game with Joseph, we go back to the technicolored coat. If there had been no coat, perhaps there would not have been so much envy and jealousy among his brothers. No jealousy, no selling to the Midianite traders. And if the Midianite traders had been headed in the opposite direction, Joseph would never have gone to Egypt. No Egypt, no selling to Potiphar. Had someone else purchased him, there would have been no encounter with Potiphar's wife. No Potiphar's wife, no prison. No prison, no meeting with the baker and the butler. No meeting with the butler, no meeting with Pharaoh to interpret his dream. No meeting with Pharaoh, and Joseph never would have become prime minister.

The game goes on. If Joseph had never become prime minister then the Jews would never have settled in the land of Goshen. Had that not occurred, there would never have been an enslavement of the Jewish people in Egypt. No slavery, no need for the rescue of a crying baby named Moses. No Moses, no Exodus. No Exodus, no Law . . . And the game continues all the way to Jesus and His redemption on the cross.

If we telescope this collection of "what ifs?" we conclude that if it were not for Joseph's technicolored coat there would be no Christianity, and every chapter of human history would have a different ending. Herein is the mystery of providential concurrence. Because God meant it for good, His servant Joseph was the victim of the envy and jealousy of his brothers.

Obviously it is conceivable that God could have worked out a different plan of salvation. He did not require Joseph's coat to get the job done. Our game of "what if?" is precisely that, a game. It makes for interesting speculation, but that is the extent of it. God doesn't play such games with human history. His providential government is serious business. What remains is that the events of Joseph's life did take place as they are written. They took place ultimately because of the perfect intentionality of God. Whatever God meant to take place, took place within the context of the mystery of concurrence.

[Chapter 10]

Primary and Secondary Causes

QUESTIONS, ALWAYS QUESTIONS . . . WE ARE CREATURES of curiosity, and we like to ask all sorts of questions. We ask, When? Where? Who? What? Perhaps the most pressing questions we ask are How? and Why? The *Why?* questions lead us ultimately to questions of metaphysics. It is said that we can exhaust any person's knowledge in any area by asking seven questions in a row, all beginning with the question "Why?" Sooner or later we will run into the simple response, "Because."

As a college senior I took a course in what was affectionately called "bonehead biology." It was a freshman-level course, biology 101. I deferred this required course until my senior year because I took Greek my freshman year, and it conflicted with the scheduling of freshman biology. By the time I was a senior I had majored in philosophy, which actually hurt me when I took the freshman class in biology, as I'll explain.

Two incidents stand out in my memory of that class. The first occurred in the first lecture, when the professor declared that matters of teleology, the doctrine that "final causes" exist, were out of bounds in the classroom. Teleology probed matters that were beyond the scope of the course, she said. I was disappointed by this declaration because, as a philosophy major, I was keenly interested in matters of teleology, and I could not understand how any scientific inquiry could afford to ignore teleological questions.

The science of teleology is concerned with purpose, ends, and goals. It focuses on the *Why?* questions. But our teacher explained that it was not ours to question "Why?" The fact that there is life is a given of biology; *why* there is life is not part of the science. Instead we were to be more concerned with the question of "How?" How does life operate? How does it act? How is it reproduced?

The second incident occurred when I missed a question on an exam. Sometimes we learn more from our errors than from our correct answers. The test question asked, "What causes a solid to change into a liquid?" I answered that the change was caused by an increase in molecular motion. The answer was marked wrong. By this time in my academic career I had formulated a policy never to challenge a grade I got on a test, sincerely believing the student was not above the teacher and that the teacher's decision on a grade was law. It was like the "law of the Medes and the Persians," not subject to change. But when I got this particular exam back and saw my answer marked wrong, I violated my policy. I really didn't care all that much about the grade, but I was confused. I thought my answer was correct, and I didn't understand why the teacher had marked it wrong. So I asked her. She explained that the correct answer to the question was "the application of heat."

When I asked her what the application of heat did to a solid, she replied, "It increases molecular motion." Now I was really confused. I reminded her that that was what I had answered on the test. She replied, "Yes, you are technically correct, but that is not the answer I was looking for." My teacher wanted the simpler answer. She wanted me to stay on the surface of the matter and not probe to the next level.

I learned an important lesson from this experience: Sometimes we deceive ourselves about our knowledge. We tend to think that if we describe what happens in certain actions we have exhaustively explained them. Description is a kind of explanation, but it is not the final resolution of questions. The more refined our descriptions, the more we are inclined to think we have answered the *Why?* questions of reality.

In the novel *The Sand Pebbles*, a humorous event takes place when a native Asian worker in the engine room of a ship explains how he keeps the engine running. He knows nothing about the science of engines; he literally plays it by ear. When the engine goes *"thumpity thump"* he knows what dials to change to correct the operation. I often feel like that. I have imagined what would happen if the entire population of the world were destroyed by a nuclear holocaust, leaving my wife and me as the sole survivors. Instantly, culture would regress to the Stone Age, at least with respect to science. For example, I have no trouble keeping my home illumined at night; it is a simple process. If I need light I just flip the light switch. The lights come on. If they don't I know to check the bulb, and if it is burned out I replace it. If that doesn't work then I check the fuse box. If no fuses are burned out, I am still not out of options to correct the situation. I simply call the power company. If all else fails, I light a candle with a match. For me, lighting is a simple matter. But don't ask me how to make a light bulb or create an electric power plant. Don't ask me how light works. I know how fast it travels, but I don't know why it travels that fast. In fact I don't really know what light is.

There are people who know a lot more about electricity and light than I do, but I suspect they go through the same basic steps that I do when the lights go out. I also suspect that for them there is still a lot of mystery about the nature of light and electricity.

The Labyrinth of Causality

I relate these matters because they are analogous to the mysteries involved in our understanding of the providence of God. We can probe the matter to various levels, but we will finally reach a point where we bump up against *Why?* and *How?* questions we simply are not able to answer. We see that there is concurrence between the action of God and the actions of human beings, but we are not sure how or why they concur.

The question of concurrence hurls us into the labyrinth of *causality,* one of the most complex issues we ever contemplate. We can make manifold distinctions in the arena of cause, such as those described as formal causes: final causes, efficient causes, material causes, and the like. These distinctions are helpful, but they are not exhaustive. Another important distinction is the distinction between *primary causality* and *secondary causality.* The Westminster Confession makes such a distinction:

> God, from all eternity, did, by the most wise and holy counsel of his own will, freely, and unchangeably ordain whatsoever comes to pass: yet so, as thereby neither is God the author of sin, nor is violence offered to the will of the creatures; nor is the liberty or contingency of *second causes* taken away, but rather established. (III/I.)

Later on we read:

> Although, in relation to the foreknowledge and decree of God, the *first Cause,* all things come to pass immutably, and infallibly; yet, by the same providence, he ordereth them to fall out, according to the nature of *second causes,* either necessarily, freely, or contingently. (V/ II.)

The distinction between first (primary) causes and second (secondary) causes is rooted in the philosophical climate of the seventeenth century, the time when the Westminster Confession was composed. The philosophers of this era were concerned with the implications evoked by the Copernican revolution and the dawning of a new age of science. Confidence in Providence was beginning to crumble in light of new discoveries of natural law. A burning question focused on how God was related to the realm of nature.

The French philosopher and mathematician René Descartes wrestled with the question of causality, particularly as it related to the question of mind and matter, thought and action. He wondered how it was possible for physical actions to give rise to ideas and how thoughts are turned into action. He defined matter in terms of what is extended. Matter, he said, has weight and measurable extension. But how big is a thought? How much does a thought weigh? We may speak of "weighty thoughts," but we do so in a figurative manner.

In his own investigation of causality, Descartes also looked at how thoughts become actions and actions produce thoughts. To illustrate Descartes's investigation, let me invite you into my study. I am writing this book on a laptop computer. I think about what words I want to write, then my fingers touch the letters on the keyboard and words appear on my screen. They aren't always spelled correctly because I often hit the wrong key. But the actual typing I am doing at this moment is a physical activity. I don't simply sit at the keyboard and think thoughts that magically appear on the screen. Physical action is necessary to transfer my thoughts into words on a page (or screen).

A moment ago somebody walked into the room and interrupted my thoughts. When I saw the person, that sight, which is an empirical perception involving my physical senses, changed my thoughts. At this point Descartes might ask, How does this work? How can an idea galvanize your fingers into typing, and how does the physical action of a person entering the room cause your thoughts to change?

Descartes answered these questions by developing a theory called *interactionism*. He speculated that the transfer between thought and action and action and thought took place at a specific point: in a gland at the base of the brain. He chose the concept of a "point" because a point in mathematics is something that is suspended between the physical and the mental, between the extended and the nonextended. A point takes up space but has no definite measurement. It is neither fish nor fowl.

Descartes's work was carried on by his students of the so-called Cartesian School. Two of these students, Malebranche and Geulincx, postulated a theory called *occasionalism*. As occasionalists, they were specifically concerned with leaving room for God in the causal nexus of the universe. They argued that there was no such thing as secondary causality. That is, there is no direct causal relationship between objects in this world. Instead, any actions, or relationships, between objects are due to the direct intervention of God.

When I pick up a shovel the thought that I have to do it does not cause it to happen. Neither is the lifting of my arms, bearing up the shovel, a direct cause. These actions, which seem to exert causal power, are merely the occasions in which God intervenes to make things happen, said the occasionalists. It is God who lifts the shovel, not me. This divine action of causality is invisible but is nevertheless real.

Other philosophers of this era took a different track. Leibniz, for example, developed a complex system of *monadology* (a monad is defined as "an unextended, indivisible, and indestructible entity that is the basic or ultimate constituent of the universe and a microcosm of it") by which he speculated that there *is* an interaction among objects that was set in motion in eternity *by God*. Leibniz spoke of the "law of preestablished harmony" that describes the causal relationships evident in nature as being preprogrammed by God in eternity. Spinoza conceived of all this in still another way, basing it on his version of substance philosophy, which was a kind of pantheistic monism.

These theories conflicted with one another and led ultimately to the skepticism of David Hume, who, working in the eighteenth century, challenged many of the assumptions tied to the law of causality. He argued that we have no way of knowing what causes what because we never have a direct perception of causality. What we experience, he said, is the customary relationships of contiguous events; we "read between the lines" and insert causal connections to these events. He illustrated this in a couple of ways. One was with his famous pool-ball analogy.

What happens in a pool game? Balls are spread on the table. We have a cue stick, a cue ball, and the numbered "object" balls. The object of the game is to "cause" certain balls to fall into certain pockets. We take the cue stick, aim it, and then exert physical action to move the stick in a motion we describe as a stroke. The tip of the cue stick strikes the cue ball. The cue ball begins to move, rolling across the felt top, and strikes the object ball. If the shot has been aimed correctly and there is no unintentional "English," or spin, imparted to the balls, the object ball rolls into the designated pocket. Voila! We score!

When we analyze all these actions we bring certain scientific laws into the discussion. Not the least of these laws is the law of inertia, which declares that objects at rest tend to remain at rest unless acted upon by an outside force. Likewise, objects in motion tend to remain in motion unless acted upon by an outside force. We start the pool game with the balls at rest and the cue stick at rest. The action of our body is the outside force that causes the cue stick to move. The motion of the cue stick then imparts force to the resting cue ball, causing it to move. At this point it is the cue stick that is the outside force that vanquishes the inertia of the resting cue ball. The force of the moving cue ball then imparts force to the object ball, causing it to move. The object ball is both acted upon and is an actor in the drama.

The skilled pool player is always concerned about where the cue ball ends up after it strikes the object ball. The player tries to exercise "cue-ball control" in order to make his next shot easier. He knows that the object ball is an outside force that has an impact on the cue ball in motion. The friction of the tabletop is also a factor as well as the angle of carom, or rebound, of the ball off a side rail.

Throughout this scenario we are assuming we have some control of the application of the laws that relate to force. We consider force vectors, angles, spin, speed, etc., as factors that enter into the game. But Hume said we don't know that any of these forces really exist. They may all be deceptive outward appearances that disguise a hidden occasionalism or some sort of preestablished harmony.

We assume there are real forces and these forces are predictable to a high degree of accuracy or in terms of what Hume called "probability quotients."

Another example of Hume's skeptical analysis involves the relationship between rain and wet grass. We see it rain, and then immediately following the rain we notice that the grass is wet. We assume that there is a causal connection between the rain falling and the grass getting wet. Hume said that all we know for sure is that we observe events that are contiguous. That is, the events touch each other in a sequence of time. Because we see such contiguous events occurring with regularity, we see a "customary relationship" between them. This does not prove that it is actually the rain that makes the grass wet. Perhaps there is an invisible imp who has a habit of wetting the grass every time it rains. This may all seem silly, but Hume had a serious purpose in mind. He was demonstrating the limits of human perceptions of external reality and the limits of empirical perception in getting to ultimate reality.

Hume has often been misunderstood. It is frequently thought that he destroyed the concept of causality altogether. He did not. It is one thing to say we cannot with certainty identify a particular cause for a particular effect. It is quite another to say that effects take place without any cause at all. To say that is to leap into irrationality. An effect, by definition, is something that has an antecedent cause. The law of causality does not say that *everything* must have a cause. If that were true then God would have to have a cause. Instead what it declares is that every *effect* must have a cause. This is analytically true because an effect is defined as the result of a cause. The law is simple: If something is an effect, then that effect must have a cause. We may not be able to identify the cause, but that is not license for us to declare that there is no cause.

The distinction between primary causality and secondary causality was designed both for scientific and theological reasons. It functions as a description but not a full explanation of the relationship between the actions of God and the actions of created things. Secondary causality refers to the force imparted by physical creatures. Primary causality refers to the causal power exerted by God in the course of cosmic events.

The Westminster divines insisted that second causes are real, that the force we exert is real force. However, any force or any power exerted in this world depends upon the power of God for its efficacy. What is behind this idea is not only the philosophical speculations of the rationalists of the seventeenth century and the empiricists of the eighteenth century but the teaching of Scripture itself. Perhaps most important is the discussion the apostle Paul had with the philosophers at Mars Hill in Athens:

> Then Paul stood in the midst of the Areopagus and said, "Men of Athens, I perceive that in all things you are very religious; for as I was passing through and considering the objects of your worship, I even found an altar with this inscription:
> TO THE UNKNOWN GOD.
> Therefore, the One whom you worship without knowing, Him I proclaim to you: God, who made the world and everything in it, since He is Lord of heaven and earth, does not dwell in temples made with hands. Nor is He worshiped with men's hands, as though He needed anything, since He gives to all life, breath, and all things. And He has made from one blood every nation of men to dwell on all the face of the earth, and has determined their preappointed times and the boundaries of their dwellings, so that they should seek the Lord, in the hope that they might grope for Him and find Him, though He is not far from each one of us; for in Him we live and move and have our being, as also some of your own poets have said, 'For we are also His offspring.'" (Acts 17:22–28)

In the ancient world of philosophy the three most difficult questions that plagued thinkers were the questions of ultimate reality (or "being"), the question of the nature of motion, and the question of the nature of life. If we were to summarize the three most complex questions for modern theoretical thought, they would still be the questions of being, motion, and life. We have made much progress since the first century, but these concepts abide as monumental enigmas.

Paul declared that "in Him [God] we live and move and have our being." God alone has the power of being within Himself. All creatures cannot be except in the being of God. Likewise, there is no power of motion or life apart from the power of God. This means that whatever causal power we exert in this world is dependent upon the power of God for its efficacy. Secondary causes are *proximate* causes. The primary, or first, cause—God—is ultimate and independent. Our causal power is derived from His power and ever contingent upon it.

The causality of God may be considered *remote* causality, as distinguished from *proximate* causality. All secondary, or proximate, causes depend upon the remote, or primary, causal power of God.

We see this relationship in the doctrine of concurrence. In the case of the drama of the life of Joseph, God was the primary and remote cause of his suffering while the actions of his brothers were the secondary and proximate causes.

This distinction is important and helpful. But we must remember that even with distinctions of this type we have not penetrated to the core of the matter. There still remains an element of mystery that conceals the secret working of the providence of God.

Chapter 11

Providence and History

THE STUDY OF HISTORY IS SOMETIMES CALLED "THE STUDY of His story." This play on words reflects the idea that all of history is the unfolding manifestation of divine providence. This was a prevailing view in the nineteenth century, when philosophers were preoccupied with devising a comprehensive philosophy of history. Hegel, for example, spoke of history as a process of collecting ideas. Marx sought to explain history in terms of the conflict of economic forces. The buzzword of the period then was *evolution*, which described history as a progressive development moving from the simple to the complex, marching inexorably toward a zenith point, or "omega point," of progress.

The nineteenth century was a period of unprecedented optimism. Faith in education and science led philosophers to believe that mankind was "coming of age," moving out of historical childhood and adolescence and toward full maturity, where disease, poverty, warfare, and social ills would all be solved. There was a relentless confidence in the innate goodness of the human spirit. Human achievement was expected to usher in a utopian world.

The outbreak of World War I at the beginning of the twentieth century burst the bubble of optimism. And even this "war to end all wars" wasn't. A Bavarian paperhanger was not pleased with the terms of the Treaty of Versailles and promised to dance a jig in Paris when Germany got its revenge and the *Lebensraum* (additional territory) he promised. He danced his jig . . . over the corpses of six million Jews. The Holocaust spawned a generation of pessimistic existential philosophers later popularized by the beatnik movement. Utopia lived up to its Greek meaning: "no place."

Sorokim of Harvard cataloged the first half of the twentieth century as the most violent century in recorded history—and that was before Vietnam, Desert Storm, Bosnia, the Palestinian wars, and a host of other international conflicts that have marked our time. By Sorokim's analysis the two most peaceful centuries of Western history were the first and the nineteenth. Philosophers began to ask if the promised evolution of human civilization was in fact a *de*volution.

The Biblical View of History

Is there a transcendent plan to world history? The Bible clearly teaches that there is. The biblical view of history stands in stark contrast to the ancient Greek view. The "God is dead" philosopher, Friedrich Nietzsche, wrote his doctoral dissertation on the conflict between two views of history in the ancient Greek world. On the one hand was the dominant view of the classical period symbolized by the Apollo figure. It was the view of *telos*, of order, harmony, and symmetry. The art of classical Greece depicted the forms of correspondence and coherence. Chaos was repudiated in favor of cosmos. On the other hand, there was the view symbolized by Dionysius. The Dionysius cult was known for its wild orgies known as Dionysian frenzies; here chaos triumphed over cosmos.

Nietzsche adopted the Dionysius model. He spoke of the victory of the "myth of eternal recurrence." This is a *cyclical* view of history, which, like the marathon dance in the movie *They Shoot Horses, Don't They?* goes round and round and round with no definite beginning and no point of termination.

This pessimistic view of history actually antedated the Greeks; it is described in the book of Ecclesiastes in the negative view of a life that is not lived "under heaven" but rather "under the sun."

"Vanity of vanities," says the Preacher;
"Vanity of vanities, all is vanity."

What profit has a man from all his labor
In which he toils under the sun?
One generation passes away, and another
    generation comes;
But the earth abides forever.
The sun also rises, and the sun goes down,
And hastens to the place where it arose.
The wind goes toward the south,
And turns around to the north;
The wind whirls about continually,
And comes again on its circuit.
All the rivers run into the sea,
Yet the sea is not full;
To the place from which the rivers come,
There they return again.
All things are full of labor;
Man cannot express it.
The eye is not satisfied with seeing,
Nor the ear filled with hearing.

That which has been is what will be,
That which is done is what will be done,
And there is nothing new under the sun. (Eccles. 1:1–9)

The tone of despair in this passage does not reflect the prevailing biblical world view. It states the perspective of the skeptic whose gaze does not reach beyond the sun. The cry "Vanity of vanities" is the credo of the nihilist who finds no ultimate meaning to human existence. It is the cry of the secularist whose life is bound by the dimensional wall of the present that has no access to eternity. The vanity mentioned is not the vanity of pride, or hubris; it is the vanity of futility. We could translate the words this way: Futility of futility, all is futility.

The emphasis on futility is linked to a view of history that is cyclical. It describes a situation in which the sun rises and the sun sets in a repetitive pattern that seems unceasing. The naturalistic skepticism that was the hallmark of Papa Hemingway is reflected in the title of one of his most important works, *The Sun Also Rises.* Likewise, the wind goes to the south and then turns back again, making a circuit. These images buttress the conclusion that there is nothing new under the sun and anticipate the Shakespearean lines:

> A poor player struts his hour upon the stage and then is heard no more. . . . It is a tale told by an idiot, full of sound and fury, signifying nothing.

The cyclical view of history is the idiot's tale. It is full of passion, of deep care and concern, but it doesn't mean anything ultimately.

This kind of pessimism is pervasive in our day. Ours is an age of secularism, and this secularism is not merely a cultural form, or a way of life. It is a world view. A. Harvey Cox explained in his book *The Secular City* that the word *secular* is derived from one of two Latin words that were used to describe the world in which we live. One of those words, *mundus*, refers to this world in its spatial dimension, the *here* of the "here and now" *(hic et nunc).* It is the word from which the English word *mundane* is derived. The other word is *saeculum*, which refers to this world in its temporal dimension. It is the *now*, or the *nunc*, of the "here and now."

The core concept of secularism has to do with history. It assumes that all of history is locked into the here and now. There is time but no eternity. There is no access to the eternal, nothing that transcends time as we experience it day to day and moment to moment. We are people who "only go around once" so we go for the gusto now because the now is all there is or ever will be. Secularism as an *ism* has no place for the providence of God in its thinking because it has no place for the eternal.

By contrast, the Hebrew concept of history is *linear*. It is not cyclical. A circle has no starting point and no end point. The linear view of history has a beginning. This is the first lesson of sacred Scripture with respect to history. The opening words of Genesis declare, "In the beginning." Thus the first three words of the Bible are on a collision course with secular views of life and the world. The fourth word is even more so, "In the beginning *God*. . . ." We don't even have to get to the fifth word, *created,* to reach the point of conflict between Christianity and secularism.

The biblical view of history starts with a beginning in time. In fact it starts with the beginning *of* time. We cannot conceive of time itself except in physical categories. We measure time by relative motion between two or more objects: a second hand moving around a dial with numbers on it or a shadow passing over the surface of a sundial or sand seeping through an hourglass. Duration is a kind of motion, and without physical objects we have no concept of motion. Time remains an enigma to us in this regard.

We use the expressions "time marches on" or "time flies" (*tempus fugit*) to refer to the chronological movement of time. The biblical view sees an endpoint, a purpose, or *telos,* to this march, or flight, of time. History has a goal, which is established in eternity by God Himself. The idea that history is meaningful and purposeful is integral to the doctrine of the providence of God.

In modern skeptical and critical views of the Bible it is often said that the "history" with which the Bible is concerned is not ordinary history but a special kind of history called *Heilsgeschicte* by the Germans. This is "salvation history" or, as it is sometimes called, *redemptive* history. With these categories at work, many have concluded that the Bible's relationship to ordinary history is either nonexistent or superfluous and that it doesn't matter whether the biblical record is accurate historically. What matters, they say, is the revelation of salvation history.

Perhaps the most important New Testament critic of the twentieth century has been Rudolf Bultmann. Bultmann, the founder of the Bultmannian School of New Testament Theology, introduced a new and radical system of interpretation of the Bible tailor-made to accommodate the Bible to modern world views. Convinced that the biblical authors worked from an antiquated and erroneous view of the world and history, Bultmann sought to establish a new theology, which he called a "theology of timelessness." Salvation, for Bultmann, is neither linear nor historical; it is *punctiliar*, occurring at a decisive point. This means salvation is not something that is wrought in space and time on the horizontal plane of world history. Rather, salvation is vertical. It occurs in a "moment," which in a way analogous to Descartes's "point" is something that takes up time but has no definite duration. How long is a moment? How many moments are there in a second? A minute? An hour? It happens "suddenly from above" in an existential encounter, a decisive moment of faith.

Bultmann ripped salvation out of its biblical and historical context. His view of history and his view of redemption are utterly foreign to biblical categories and reflect more of an existential revision of Christianity than biblical faith. Historic Christianity stands or falls with its tie to ordinary history. Dutch New Testament scholar Hermann Ridderbos once remarked that though it is true that biblical history is *redemptive* history, it is also redemptive *history*.

Perhaps Bultmann's most vigorous critic was the European scholar Oscar Cullmann. Cullmann wrote three books, a polemical trilogy aimed chiefly at Bultmann. The first of these was entitled *Christus und der Zeit*, or *Christ and Time*. In this volume Cullmann explored the various words used in the New Testament with respect to references to time. He examined Jesus' use of the term *hour* as He frequently referred to His hour that had "not yet come." He pointed out the significance of two Greek words, *chronos* and *kairos*, that can be and have been translated by the English word *time*.

The term *chronos* refers to the ordinary moment-to-moment

passing of time. It captures what we call "chronology." We get words like *chronicle* or *chronometer* from this Greek term. The word *kairos* is a bit more exotic. We do not have an exact corresponding term for it in English. The closest I can come to it is the English word *historic*. We can make a distinction between the historic and the historical. Everything that happens in time is historical, but not everything that occurs in time is historic. We reserve the word *historic* for events that are of crucial import for history, that appear to change or alter the course of history. For example, the signing of the Declaration of Independence was not only an historical event in American history, it was an historic event. Likewise such events as the stock market crash, the bombing of Pearl Harbor, and the assassination of John F. Kennedy were historic events.

In the New Testament, a *kairotic* event is one that is pregnant in significance. It is a moment in which the past reaches a point of culmination and has determining significance for everything that follows after it. The birth of Christ was such an event, as were His baptism, crucifixion, resurrection, and ascension, as well as the events that occurred at Pentecost. In the Old Testament the Flood and the Exodus would be considered *kairotic* events. These events are "loaded" with redemptive historical significance and reveal something of God's purpose in history. God's work of redemption takes place in and through the arena of history. A *kairos* is not something that is trans-historical. It does not take place in some *noumenal,* or mythical, realm. It takes place in real time and in real places involving real people. This is the fundamental difference between history and myth. As critics of Cullmann have pointed out, the Bible is not a book of mythology. Jewish religion is already demythologized and differs markedly from other ancient mythic religions in its approach to sober history. The Greeks didn't care if Athena really was born *de novo* (anew) from the head of Zeus as a matter of historical record. Christianity *does* care whether Jesus really was the incarnation of God in history and if He really did rise from the dead in space and time. Peter said it this way:

For we did not follow cunningly devised fables when we made known to you the power and coming of our Lord Jesus Christ, but were eyewitnesses of His majesty. For He received from God the Father honor and glory when such a voice came to Him from the Excellent Glory: "This is My beloved Son, in whom I am well pleased." And we heard this voice which came from heaven when we were with Him on the holy mountain.

And so we have the prophetic word confirmed, which you do well to heed as a light that shines in a dark place, until the day dawns and the morning star rises in your hearts. (2 Pet. 1:16-19)

The New Testament writers sought to give an account of what they saw with their eyes and heard with their ears. They stood in sharp contrast to the writers of Gnostic literature who avoided knowledge received via the senses. The New Testament is not a Gnostic book. It is a record that purports to declare what really happened in space and time.

The idea of *kairos* concerns not only pregnant moments in history but also the end, or consummation, of history. It deals not only with things that have occurred, with things past, but also with things that have not yet happened, with things future. We see this in an interesting encounter that Jesus has with a demon:

When He had come to the other side, to the country of the Gergesenes, there met Him two demon-possessed men, coming out of the tombs, exceedingly fierce, so that no one could pass that way. And suddenly they cried out, saying, "What have we to do with You, Jesus, You Son of God? Have You come here to torment us before the time?"

Now a good way off from them there was a herd of many swine feeding. So the demons begged Him, saying, "If You cast us out, permit us to go away into the herd of swine."

And He said to them, "Go." So when they had come out, they went into the herd of swine. And suddenly the whole herd of swine ran violently down the steep place into the sea, and perished in the water.

Then those who kept them fled; and they went away into the city and told everything, including what had happened to the demon-possessed men. (Matt. 8:28-33)

At first glance this passage seems to suggest that Jesus negotiated with demons. They recognized Him as the Son of God and complained that He would torment them "before the time." The word in the Greek text is *kairos*. The demons evidently knew that God had appointed a particular time, a *kairotic* moment in the future, when they would be subject to divine wrath and torment, presumably when they were destined to be cast into the pit of hell. They also knew that although all authority on heaven and earth had been given to the Son of God, that authority did not include changing the timetable for future events established in eternity by the Father.

In any case, Jesus did not send the demons to hell. My guess is that He did not do this precisely because the demons were correct. It was not the time, or the *kairos*, for this. He did cast the demons out of the men. It was the time for these men's redemption and release from the torment they experienced at the hands of the demons. It was their time for redemption but not the time for the demons' ultimate punishment.

Some (perhaps they were animal rights activists) have complained that Jesus caused needless suffering for innocent pigs by sending the demons into them. This accusation forgets the order of creation and the role mankind plays as vice regent in God's world. We have been given dominion over the animal kingdom. Of course this is not a license for abusing animals, but in this case Jesus used the pigs as instruments of redemption for two human beings. This was not the first time in Jewish history when animals were sacrificed for the sake of mankind. The principle was deeply rooted in the sacrificial system of the Old Testament.

(We might also ask what a farmer in this region was doing herding swine, since pigs were considered unclean animals.) No, the demons were not unfairly punished; they were forced to submit to the authority of Jesus and had to obey His command to leave the men.

All moments of history, the entire chronology of time, are in the hands of and under the supervision of Providence. The specific moments of *kairotic* events are rich, not only in their redemptive value, but in their revelatory value as well. The specific bears witness to the general. The events of redemption that happen within the framework of ordinary history give us the deeper assurance that all of history is in His hands. It means the crisis moments in our own lives are not expressions of vanity or futility. The tale of history is not left to idiots.

The Bible is concerned with a time that is moving in an appointed direction. Times do matter. The former times have passed away, and we currently live in the "last times." The present time is a time of crisis for the world, a time in which every moment counts forever. It is the time when all men everywhere are called by God to repent and embrace Christ, as Paul declared at Mars Hill:

"Truly, these times of ignorance God overlooked, but now commands all men everywhere to repent, because He has appointed a day on which He will judge the world in righteousness by the Man whom He has ordained. He has given assurance of this to all by raising Him from the dead." (Acts 17:30-31)

Chapter 12

The Intersection of Redemptive and Secular History

REDEMPTIVE HISTORY TAKES PLACE WITHIN THE CONTEXT of ordinary history; it occurs in real time and space. To be sure, however, there is a transcendent and vertical dimension to it. In redemptive history the eternal intersects the temporal; eternity intersects time; the infinite touches the finite. Because the two touch, it is improper to view them in terms of radical discontinuity.

The life of Christ begins in the framework of world history:

> And it came to pass in those days that a decree went out from Caesar Augustus that all the world should be registered. This census first took place while Quirinius was governing Syria. So all went to be registered, everyone to his own city.
>
> Joseph also went up from Galilee, out of the city of Nazareth, into Judea, to the city of David, which is called Bethlehem, because he was of the house and lineage of David, to be registered with Mary, his betrothed wife, who was with child. So it was, that while they were there, the days were completed for her to be delivered. And she brought forth her firstborn Son, and wrapped Him in swaddling cloths, and laid Him in a manger, because there was no room for them in the inn. (Luke 2:1–7)

Jesus was born during the *Pax Romana*, the zenith of Roman culture and conquest. Emperor Augustus Caesar had ascended the throne. After the internecine struggle between the famous triumvirates, and after Julius Caesar had been assassinated at the feet of the bust of Pompey, the young and gifted Octavian took the Roman government to unprecedented heights.

The Roman Empire had introduced a system of communication designed to facilitate the movement of its armies; this system of roads linking the parts of the empire was the envy of the world. The roads were designed, engineered, and constructed with such efficiency that some of them survive even to this day. In addition, the Romans developed an efficient postal system that perhaps should be copied by the American government.

It is impossible to conceive of the rapid expansion of the early Christian church apart from these cultural advantages. The gospel was carried to the known world over Roman roads and via the Roman postal system. Much of the New Testament is a result of letters, or epistles, that were written and circulated via this system.

From time to time the Roman government took a census for the chief purpose of taxation. Residents were required to enroll at the place of their birth, a requirement that sometimes necessitated arduous travel. It was during such an enrollment that Jesus was born, fulfilling what the prophet Micah had prophesied centuries earlier as to the geographical site of the future Messiah's birthplace:

> "But you, Bethlehem Ephrathah,
> Though you are little among the thousands of Judah,
> Yet out of you shall come forth to Me
> The One to be Ruler in Israel,
> Whose goings forth are from of old,
> From everlasting."
>
> Therefore He shall give them up,
> Until the time that she who is in labor has given birth;
> Then the remnant of His brethren

Shall return to the children of Israel.
And He shall stand and feed His flock
In the strength of the LORD,
In the majesty of the name of the LORD His God;
And they shall abide,
For now He shall be great
To the ends of the earth. (Micah 5:2–4)

The tiny village of Bethlehem, the city of David, was selected by God to be the birthplace of the Messiah. But Joseph and his betrothed wife, Mary, lived in Nazareth, a circumstance that had prompted Nathaniel to ask, "Can any good thing come out of Nazareth?" The New Testament does not regard the birth of Jesus in Bethlehem as a fortuitous accident of history. It was not by chance that the decree of Augustus Caesar forced Mary and Joseph to journey to this village. Behind the political power of Caesar was the transcendent providence of God. Completely unknown to Augustus himself, his decree was but a tool in the hand of God to ensure that the truth of Old Testament prophecy be made manifest and that His Word would come to pass.

Scripture declares that Jesus was born in the "fullness of time." The word that is translated "fullness" is the Greek word *pleroma*. The English word *fullness* does not quite capture the meaning of this word. *Pleroma* refers to a fullness that is absolute, a fullness that reaches its bursting point. When we fill a glass of water, we do not fill it to the rim. A small, empty space is left lest we spill the contents when we lift the glass to drink. The fullness of *pleroma* would be more like what happens when we put the glass under a spigot and turn on the water and let it run. The glass fills up and then begins to spill over the side. In this case there is no room left in the glass for any more water.

The "fullness of time" means that history was ripe for the birth of Christ. All of the *chronos* of the past and all of the *kairoi* that had gone before converged in this moment. Jesus was born at the precise second and in the precise place that God had ordained from the foundation of the world. Luke records it with these words: "So it was, that while they were there, the days were completed for her to be delivered." But it was not only the days of Mary's pregnancy, the normal period of gestation, that was completed. It was the years, centuries, and millennia that had been completed in preparation for this moment.

Luke's reference to Caesar Augustus and to Quirinius, governor of Syria, place the incarnation account squarely in the context of secular history. Providence caused the meeting of primary and secondary causes, secular and redemptive history.

But it was not only Christ's birth that is placed within the record of secular history; His death also took place in the fullness of time. The Apostles' Creed makes no mention of Augustus, but it does make reference to another historical figure, the Roman official Pontius Pilate, the procurator of Jerusalem. The phrase "suffered under Pontius Pilate" is recited by thousands of people every week. Why is Pilate singled out for this mention? Why not Herod or Caiaphas? Historians and theologians have speculated that Pilate exercised a unique role in redemptive history. It was he who pronounced the death sentence on Jesus. He was the Gentile ruler who condemned the Messiah, fulfilling the prophecy that the Messiah would be "delivered into the hands of the Gentiles."

Pilate exercised the role of *publica persona*, but he was more than just a run-of-the-mill public official. He was appointed by God in His providence to pronounce judgment upon Christ. The New Testament labors the point that no one was able to *take* Christ's life from Him; Jesus was actively involved in laying down His life for His sheep. In light of this, Jesus had an interesting interchange with Pilate regarding Pilate's authority:

> Then Pilate said to Him, "Are You not speaking to me? Do You not know that I have power to crucify You, and power to release You?"
>
> Jesus answered, "You could have no power at all against Me unless it had been given you from above. Therefore the one who delivered Me to you has the greater sin." (John 19:10–11)

Jesus challenged Pilate's claim to have power or authority over Him. Jesus said, "You *could have no power* . . . *unless*. . . ." The word *could* here refers to human ability. The word *unless* points to a necessary condition that must be met before something can happen. These words indicate that Pilate's power or authority was dependent upon a necessary condition. That condition was the giving of that power or authority by God.

During the interrogation of Jesus by Pilate, their conversation had Pilate uttering words that carried far more meaning than he possibly could have realized:

> Then Pilate entered the Praetorium again, called Jesus, and said to Him, "Are You the King of the Jews?"
>
> Jesus answered him, "Are you speaking for yourself about this, or did others tell you this concerning Me?"
>
> Pilate answered, "Am I a Jew? Your own nation and the chief priests have delivered You to me. What have You done?"
>
> Jesus answered, "My kingdom is not of this world. If My kingdom were of this world, My servants would fight, so that I should not be delivered to the Jews; but now My kingdom is not from here."
>
> Pilate therefore said to Him, "Are You a king then?"
>
> Jesus answered, "You say rightly that I am a king. For this cause I was born, and for this cause I have come into the world, that I should bear witness to the truth. Everyone who is of the truth hears My voice."
>
> Pilate said to Him, "What is truth?" And when he had said this, he went out again to the Jews, and said to them, "I find no fault in Him at all." (John 18:33–38)

Jesus was a king, but not in the sense that Pilate understood the term. After this exchange Pilate's declaration to the crowd, "I find no fault in the man," was his official judgment as the *publica persona*. But it was more than that. Again Pilate had no idea how true his judgment was. He couldn't find any fault in the man because there was no fault to be found in Him. Obviously Pilate's judgment was a restricted one. He was simply declaring that he could find no violation of Roman law in Jesus that would warrant or justify His crucifixion. But in a deeper and broader sense Pilate was speaking the judgment of God. There was absolutely no fault in this man, neither from the scrutiny of Roman law nor from the scrutiny of divine law. This was the sinless One who stood before Pilate, the Lamb without blemish who was being readied for the slaughter.

Pilate made another statement regarding Christ, which on the surface appears innocuous:

> So then Pilate took Jesus and scourged Him. And the soldiers twisted a crown of thorns and put it on His head, and they put on Him a purple robe. Then they said, "Hail, King of the Jews!" And they struck Him with their hands.
>
> Pilate then went out again, and said to them, "Behold, I am bringing Him out to you, that you may know that I find no fault in Him."
>
> Then Jesus came out, wearing the crown of thorns and the purple robe. And Pilate said to them, "Behold the Man!" (John 19:1–5)

The phrase "Behold the Man" in Latin was uttered as *"ecce homo."* It may seem strange that these two words have received the attention they have in church history. In its context it appears to be simply a part of the mockery to which Jesus was subjected. His captors dressed Him in the mock garments of a king, belittling the ascription of royalty to Him. Pilate's words simply mean, "Look at the man." But theologians of antiquity saw in this another example of an unintentional double meaning provoked by Providence. When Jesus was put on display before the watching world, He was not presented as God but as "the man." Indeed this was not merely *a* man standing there. It was *the* Man. This One was the embodiment of a new humanity, the Second Adam, the Man who perfectly fulfilled the purpose of human creation, to mirror and reflect the character of God by bearing His divine image. As the author of Hebrews declared:

God, who at various times and in various ways spoke in time past to the fathers by the prophets, has in these last days spoken to us by His Son, whom He has appointed heir of all things, through whom also He made the worlds; who being the brightness of His glory and the express image of His person, and upholding all things by the word of His power, when He had by Himself purged our sins, sat down at the right hand of the Majesty on high. (Heb. 1:1–3)

Note that Jesus is described as the "brightness" of God's glory and "the express image of His person." This He was, not only in His deity, but also in His humanity. Pilate's call to the world to behold this man is counsel that transcends his intended mockery.

In birth, life, and death Jesus carries out the redemptive purpose of God on the plane of human history. It is ironic that all of secular history is measured by reference to Him. I am writing this book in 1995. These numbers might have the initials A.D. added to them. The A.D. refers to the Latin *anno domine,* or "the year of our Lord." All of history is framed around this Person who came in the fullness of time and whose coming gives definition to all of time.

Esther's Moment of Destiny

Another example of the intersection of redemptive history with secular history may be seen in the narrative history of Esther. The book of Esther is somewhat strange. Some have argued that it does not even belong in the canon of sacred Scripture because it seems more like a chapter in the secular history of the Persian Empire than it does a chapter in Old Testament revelation. Some scholars have said the book appears to be a-theological because it doesn't focus upon God.

On the contrary! The book of Esther is filled to the brim with God as it reflects a chapter in the history of His invisible hand of Providence. The book begins with a reference to secular history:

Now it came to pass in the days of Ahasuerus (this was the Ahasuerus who reigned over one hundred and twenty-seven provinces, from India to Ethiopia), in those days when King Ahasuerus sat on the throne of his kingdom, which was in Shushan the citadel, that in the third year of his reign he made a feast for all his officials and servants—the powers of Persia and Media, the nobles, and the princes of the provinces being before him—when he showed the riches of his glorious kingdom and the splendor of his excellent majesty for many days, one hundred and eighty days in all.

And when these days were completed, the king made a feast lasting seven days for all the people who were present in Shushan the citadel, from great to small, in the court of the garden of the king's palace. (Esther 1:1–5)

On the occasion of this great feast the king summoned his queen, Vashti, to present herself to the dignitaries assembled. His purpose was to put her beauty on display to the people and the officials. It was clearly an act of pride on the part of Ahasuerus. But Vashti refused to come, defying the king's command, provoking his rage and fury. His ego had been assaulted, and his authority challenged. The king sought counsel from his sages to determine how to deal with his obstreperous queen. The answer reflected the insecurity of all the men gathered there:

And Memucan answered before the king and the princes: "Queen Vashti has not only wronged the king, but also all the princes, and all the people who are in all the provinces of King Ahasuerus. For the queen's behavior will become known to all women, so that they will despise their husbands in their eyes, when they report, 'King Ahasuerus commanded Queen Vashti to be brought in before him, but she did not come.' This very day the noble ladies of Persia and Media will say to all the king's officials that they have heard of the behavior of the queen. Thus there will be excessive contempt and wrath. If it pleases the king, let a royal decree go out from him, and let it be recorded in the laws of the Persians and the Medes, so that it will not be altered, that Vashti shall come no more before King

Ahasuerus; and let the king give her royal position to another who is better than she." (Esther 1:16–19)

What followed was an attempt to find a suitable replacement for Vashti as queen. A spectacular beauty pageant was held throughout the kingdom as a search was undertaken to find a virgin beautiful enough to please the king. It was like a chapter out of Cinderella.

In the kingdom resided Mordecai, a Jew who had been among those carried away in the Babylonian captivity. His uncle's daughter had been left orphaned by the death of her father and mother, and Mordecai had taken her under his care and treated her as his own daughter. Her name was Esther. As a result of the massive beauty pageant, Esther was chosen to be the new queen. Mordecai instructed her not to reveal her ethnic identity, not to disclose that a Jewess had risen to the rank of queen of the Persians.

It so happened that the king elevated a man named Haman to a rank above all the princes of Persia, commanding that all the servants pay homage to him. But because of his Jewish convictions, Mordecai refused to bow down before Haman. In his furious quest for revenge against Mordecai, Haman sought not only to punish him but all the Jews in the land. Haman proposed to Ahasuerus that the king issue a decree to destroy all the Jews in the empire, and Haman personally offered a reward of ten thousand talents of silver to those who would carry out the decree. This was an attempt at genocide, a threat of holocaust against the Jews.

An edict from the king was the "law of the Medes and the Persians," meaning it could not be repealed; it was irrevocable. When the Jews heard of it, there was great fear and mourning among them; they considered their situation to be hopeless. Mordecai tore his clothes and put on sackcloth and ashes. Then, in desperation, he sent a message to Esther, calling on her to intercede for her people. Esther's initial response was less than heroic:

"All the king's servants and the people of the king's provinces know that any man or woman who goes into the inner court to the king, who has not been called, he has but one law: put all to death, except the one to whom the king holds out the golden scepter, that he may live. Yet I myself have not been called to go in to the king these thirty days."(Esther 4:11)

When Mordecai received this message he was distressed. He shot off a reply to Esther, calling upon her to consider the gravity of the situation and to consider her role in history:

> And Mordecai told them to answer Esther: "Do not think in your heart that you will escape in the king's palace any more than all the other Jews. For if you remain completely silent at this time, relief and deliverance will arise for the Jews from another place, but you and your father's house will perish. Yet who knows whether you have come to the kingdom for such a time as this?" (Esther 4:13–14)

Mordecai's reply and charge to Esther was done with a view to the providence of God. He warned her that she would not escape the purge of the Jews and then raised the crucial question: "Who knows whether you have come to the kingdom for such a time as this?" The words "such a time as this" drip with a sense of providence. This was a time of crisis, a *kairotic* moment in the history of Israel. It was a time for divine intervention when God would use a human agent to bring about His deliverance of His people. It was Esther's moment of destiny, the moment for which she was born.

Esther's second response was radically different from her first. She took seriously her vocation and said:

> "Go, gather all the Jews who are present in Shushan, and fast for me; neither eat nor drink for three days, night or day. My maids and I will fast likewise. And so I will go to the king, which is against the law; and if I perish, I perish!" (Esther 4:16)

With these words Esther threw herself into the hands of Providence. She understood the law of the Medes and the Persians.

She was familiar with the fate of queens like Vashti who dared to defy the mandate of the king. But she determined to act in behalf of her people anyway, hoping against hope that she would succeed:

> Now it happened on the third day that Esther put on her royal robes and stood in the inner court of the king's palace, across from the king's house, while the king sat on his royal throne in the royal house, facing the entrance of the house. So it was, when the king saw Queen Esther standing in the court, that she found favor in his sight, and the king held out to Esther the golden scepter that was in his hand. Then Esther went near and touched the top of the scepter.
>
> And the king said to her, "What do you wish, Queen Esther? What is your request? It shall be given to you—up to half the kingdom!" (Esther 5:1–3)

The queen had come to the inner court of the palace when she had not been summoned. She did this at the risk of provoking the king's fury. She awaited his response. When the king extended the royal scepter to her, it was the sign of his approval. The audience was granted. Esther then asked the king to come to a banquet she had prepared for him and for Haman. In the meantime Haman had prepared a gallows in order to hang Mordecai. At the banquet Ahasuerus asked Esther for her petition, stating his willingness to grant her up to half the kingdom:

> Then Queen Esther answered and said, "If I have found favor in your sight, O king, and if it pleases the king, let my life be given me at my petition, and my people at my request. For we have been sold, my people and I, to be destroyed, to be killed, and to be annihilated. Had we been sold as male and female slaves, I would have held my tongue, although the enemy could never compensate for the king's loss."
>
> So King Ahasuerus answered and said to Queen Esther, "Who is he, and where is he, who would dare presume in his heart to do such a thing?"

And Esther said, "The adversary and enemy is this wicked Haman!"

So Haman was terrified before the king and queen. (Esther 7:3–6)

When Esther explained the wicked machinations of Haman, the law of the Medes and the Persians was altered. The decree against the Jews was rescinded, and Haman was hanged on the gallows he had prepared for Mordecai. Esther had done what she was called to do. Redemptive history intruded into the history of the Persians, and the intersection of the divine and the human accomplished the rescue of the Jews.

Chapter 13

Providence and the Church

I WAS A GUEST PREACHER IN A CHURCH LAST SUNDAY.
The congregation numbered about 150 persons. When I stepped
into the pulpit I mentioned that I was intimidated when I had to
give a sermon in the presence of millions of people. The congregation looked at me in bewilderment as there were no television
cameras present to broadcast this sermon beyond the hearing of
those present. I explained that when we gathered as the people of
God, our worship was in the presence of all the host of heaven, all
the angels and archangels. Not only that, but we were assembled
with the entire communion of saints (*communio sanctorum*), with
those believers who have gone before us into heaven. In addition,
we were gathered in that particular place at the same time millions
of others were gathered for worship around the world.

When the people of God gather for worship, there is an intersection between time and eternity, between heaven and earth. This
point should not be a novelty in our understanding because it is
written large in the pages of Scripture. Consider the exposition of
the author of Hebrews:

> For you have not come to the mountain that may be touched and
> that burned with fire, and to blackness and darkness and tempest,

and the sound of a trumpet and the voice of words, so that those who heard it begged that the word should not be spoken to them anymore. (For they could not endure what was commanded: "And if so much as a beast touches the mountain, it shall be stoned or shot with an arrow." And so terrifying was the sight that Moses said, "I am exceedingly afraid and trembling.")

But you have come to Mount Zion and to the city of the living God, the heavenly Jerusalem, to an innumerable company of angels, to the general assembly and church of the firstborn who are registered in heaven, to God the Judge of all, to the spirits of just men made perfect, to Jesus the Mediator of the new covenant, and to the blood of sprinkling that speaks better things than that of Abel. (Heb. 12:18–24)

Here the author alludes to the assembly of Israel at Sinai in the Old Testament, a moment of supreme dread and terror. The people had been consecrated for this event and warned not to go up the mountain or even touch its base on penalty of death. For three days they waited in anticipation of the event:

Then it came to pass on the third day, in the morning, that there were thunderings and lightnings, and a thick cloud on the mountain; and the sound of the trumpet was very loud, so that all the people who were in the camp trembled. And Moses brought the people out of the camp to meet with God, and they stood at the foot of the mountain. Now Mount Sinai was completely in smoke, because the LORD descended upon it in fire. Its smoke ascended like the smoke of a furnace, and the whole mountain quaked greatly. And when the blast of the trumpet sounded long and became louder and louder, Moses spoke, and God answered him by voice. Then the LORD came down upon Mount Sinai, on the top of the mountain. And the LORD called Moses to the top of the mountain, and Moses went up.

And the LORD said to Moses, "Go down and warn the people, lest they break through to gaze at the LORD, and many of them perish.

Also let the priests who come near the LORD consecrate themselves, lest the LORD break out against them." (Exod. 19:16–22)

This was when Moses went up on Mount Sinai to meet with God and to receive the Decalogue from His hand. At Sinai God manifested His presence, an event punctuated by the sight of a thick cloud that concealed God from the eyes of the people, by thunder and the loud blaring of the trumpet. It was most unlike what is experienced in the normal Sunday church service of today.

Next the assembly focused on the meeting of God with His people at the tabernacle and then later in the temple. The tabernacle was called the "Tent of Meeting." It was portable so that wherever the people went in their wanderings God would go with them. When the twelve tribes encamped they pitched their tribal tents in a circle, and the tabernacle was then pitched in the middle to indicate that God was in their midst. But God was not only among them; He pledged to "go before them" to lead them in the wilderness. Later, when the temple was built to serve as their central sanctuary, the people would customarily "go up to Zion" to meet with God.

But when the New Testament was written, things changed. The time for temple worship was over. The priesthood of Aaron was over. The rites of the sacrificial system of the Old Testament had reached their culmination in the priestly work of Christ. A new order had been established; a new covenant had been ratified. The old system was but a shadow of things to come. With the crucifixion of Christ, the veil of the temple had been rent.

The book of Hebrews was written shortly before A.D. 70, when the temple was destroyed and the cultic practices of Israel ended. The old was passing away, being replaced by an entire new system.

The language and imagery of the New Testament reference saying the old system was merely the "shadow" of things to come are reminiscent of the language of Plato. This is not to suggest that the New Testament is but warmed-over Platonism. Far from it! Yet the parallel to certain aspects of Plato's thought is obvious. In Plato's

"Theory of Ideas" the realm of ultimate reality was conceived of in terms of the ideal realm of eternal reality. The physical realm of earth was conceived of as the realm of *receptacles*. Plato defined a receptacle as an imperfect copy of the eternal ideal. For Plato all physical things were shadows of the real, like the shadows on the wall in his famous cave analogy. What Plato didn't conceive of was the real presence of the ideal in the physical world. He had no room for the incarnation of God in history.

The biblical categories are not Platonic, yet the Bible does speak of shadows. These shadows have a vital role to play in the history of redemption. They serve as precursors, or pointers, to the reality that was to come in real history. The reality came in Christ. Plato was never able to escape the tension of dualism that separated heaven and earth.

In Christ we have the ladder, or bridge, that connects the eternal with the temporal. In His priestly work He bridges the gap between heaven and earth; His priestly work is accomplished on earth, yet it gives His people access to the heavenly realm. Paul speaks of this in his letter to the Ephesians:

Blessed be the God and Father of our Lord Jesus Christ, who has blessed us with every spiritual blessing in the heavenly places in Christ, just as He chose us in Him before the foundation of the world, that we should be holy and without blame before Him in love, having predestined us to adoption as sons by Jesus Christ to Himself, according to the good pleasure of His will, to the praise of the glory of His grace, by which He made us accepted in the Beloved.

In Him we have redemption through His blood, the forgiveness of sins, according to the riches of His grace which He made to abound toward us in all wisdom and prudence, having made known to us the mystery of His will, according to His good pleasure which He purposed in Himself, that in the dispensation of the fullness of the times He might gather together in one all things in Christ, both which are in heaven and which are on earth—in Him. (Eph. 1:3–10)

These words are somewhat mysterious to us. They point to the finished work of Christ by which, after making His atonement, He entered into the heavenly sanctuary, into the transcendent temple, and gave access for His people in heaven. There is a mystical aspect to our union with Christ. The church is His mystical body; when we gather for worship He is in our midst, and we are made present in the heavenly places with Him. Worship for the people of God is now a taste of heaven itself. In our earthly assembly we celebrate the intersection between ordinary history and redemptive history. This intersection is invisible to us but is nevertheless real.

The Invisible Church

In the history of theology a distinction is made between the *visible church* and the *invisible church*. This distinction, which received prominence in the thought of Augustine, is important for more than one reason. In the first place, it calls attention to the fact that the visible church on earth contains people who are not truly numbered among the elect. The earthly church contains tares along with the wheat. It is what Augustine described as a *corpus per mixtum*, a "mixed body" of believers and unbelievers. Not every person who makes a profession of faith actually has the faith he or she professes. Jesus warned of those who would honor Him with their lips while their hearts would be far from Him. He warned that on the day of judgment people will call out, saying "Lord, Lord" and He will respond with the blood-curdling words, "Depart from Me . . . I never knew you."

The invisible church is called invisible because it is invisible to our eyes. Only God can read the hearts of people. We look on the outward appearances while God examines the heart. The church is never invisible to God. It is clearly known within His purview. For Augustine the distinction did not separate groups or people. He argued that the invisible church exists essentially and substantially *within* the visible church. Likewise, Calvin maintained that it was the task of the people of God, the true believers, to make the invisible church visible by their worship and service.

But there is another sense in which the church is invisible. This is the sense in which we cannot see the broader congregation of its members who are already in heaven. This is the church that is no longer found at the base of Mount Sinai or in the earthly temple in Jerusalem. It is the church that now resides in the city of the living God, the heavenly Jerusalem. This is the church that includes the innumerable company of angels, the general assembly, and the church of the firstborn who are registered in heaven. It is the church that includes the spirits of just men made perfect.

In light of the innumerable references to this heavenly dimension of the church, it is strange indeed that this idea remains so foreign to our thinking. We seem to be stuck with the kind of thinking that was evident in the woman at the well:

> The woman said to Him, "Sir, I perceive that You are a prophet. Our fathers worshiped on this mountain, and you Jews say that in Jerusalem is the place where one ought to worship."
>
> Jesus said to her, "Woman, believe Me, the hour is coming when you will neither on this mountain, nor in Jerusalem, worship the Father. You worship what you do not know; we know what we worship, for salvation is of the Jews. But the hour is coming, and now is, when the true worshipers will worship the Father in spirit and truth; for the Father is seeking such to worship Him. God is Spirit, and those who worship Him must worship in spirit and truth." (John 4:19–24)

The woman of Sychar was convinced that the worship of God was a local matter. The dispute between the Jews and the Samaritans focused upon the question of *where* it was proper to worship God, in Jerusalem or at Mount Gerizim. This did not reflect a Jewish belief in the restricted presence of God as if He were not omnipresent. The question of "Where?" was not so much a question of where God was but rather where the church was to be gathered for worship. It involved a question of where God would *meet* with His people.

Jesus' answer to the woman's question was deeper than what appears simply on the surface. That God is a Spirit was no new insight. Jesus did not say, "God is a Spirit; therefore He is not contained in His presence to either Gerizim or Jerusalem," although that would certainly be true enough. Jesus clearly understood the axiom Calvin would express as *finitum non capax infinitum*, the finite cannot contain the infinite. Rather, Jesus was directing His comments more to the question of the "How?" of worship. Since God is a Spirit, it is proper to worship Him "in spirit." True worship is spiritual worship; it is also to be done "in truth." The worship of the people of God was about to undergo a significant change. Jesus said that an hour was approaching, indeed had already arrived, that ushered in a new kind of worship. Again, this did not mean that in the Old Testament worship was not to be spiritual or according to truth.

With the incarnation of Christ, the Great High Priest was on the earth. The old was passing away. The curtain in the temple would soon be rent, and the temple itself was soon to be destroyed. Our Messiah was about to enter into the heavenly sanctuary and open its doors for the communion of saints.

God cares for His church with a special providence. From the cry of Abel's blood from the earth, through the Exodus and exile, He preserved His remnant by His providential care. The church of the new covenant would be established upon a new foundation, the foundation of the apostles, which stood not over against but along with the foundation of the Old Testament prophets. The new did not destroy the old but built upon it. It was given a special praise of providential care:

> He said to them, "But who do you say that I am?"
> Simon Peter answered and said, "You are the Christ, the Son of the living God."
> Jesus answered and said to him, "Blessed are you, Simon Bar-Jonah, for flesh and blood has not revealed this to you, but My

Father who is in heaven. And I also say to you that you are Peter, and on this rock I will build My church, and the gates of Hades shall not prevail against it. And I will give you the keys of the kingdom of heaven, and whatever you bind on earth will be bound in heaven, and whatever you loose on earth will be loosed in heaven." (Matt. 16:15–19)

Jesus called Simon *Petros*, or "the rock," declaring that He would build His church upon this rock. The tendency in church history is for the Roman Catholic Church to read too much into this designation and for Protestants to see too little. Jesus did not here establish a papacy, but He did point to the apostolic foundation upon which He was building His church.

Jesus also declared that the gates of hell would not prevail against His church. What does this mean? This is not an easy statement to interpret because it can have more than one meaning. In the first instance the reference to gates means the entrances to strongholds. In the ancient world, large cities were surrounded by high walls. These were fortified cities, built to withstand attacks from hostile forces. The city gates were often mammoth in size and weight, built to withstand assault by battering rams. In this sense the gates were *defensive* structures. To say then that the gates of hell would not prevail against the church may mean that the church is called to be an *offensive* force, invading the world with the power of the gospel, which cannot be withstood by the strongholds of hell.

Another possibility, which I think is less likely, is that the reference to the gates of hell may refer to the source from which emerges satanic forces that aggressively assault the church. In this case it is the forces of hell that are on the attack, and the church is on the defensive against them. In this interpretation we have the promise of Christ that the church will never be vanquished by evil.

I am not sure which of these views Jesus had in mind when He made His statement to Simon Peter. One thing is clear, however; both interpretations express a sound view of God's promises to His church. Certainly the New Testament makes it clear that the offensive power of the gospel is greater than the strongholds of hell. It is equally true that God so protects His church that it will never be vanquished from the earth. Modern historians who have declared this to be the post-Christian era in which God is dead and the church is His mausoleum have been premature in their obituaries. The church is not dead because it cannot die. Individual parishes may disappear, and whole denominations may become apostate, but the invisible church is impregnable and will always have some visible manifestation on earth.

Because of the providence of God, no Christian can ever afford to be, or be justified in being, pessimistic with respect to the future of the church. The church may go through dark periods when its light seems to fade and its flame begin to cool, but the Lord of the church has so subjected His body to His care that it cannot die.

It has been said that the church is the most corrupt institution on earth. That may be true from the perspective of evaluating institutions in terms of their gifts and relative responsibilities. We know that of those to whom much has been given, much will be required—and no institution has been so richly gifted by divine grace than the church. If our sin is measured against this backdrop, then perhaps the church *is* the most corrupt institution on earth. But at the same time this institution, which is populated by sinners, is also the most holy institution on earth. The church is holy because it has been consecrated unto a holy task and because its members (at least in the case of the invisible church) have been indwelt by the Holy Spirit. The church on earth has spots and wrinkles, but these blemishes are being made clean as Christ adorns His bride for her future wedding feast with Him. The church is not the only place where God's providence is at work, as we have said, but it is the place where the means of grace are most clearly concentrated. As God steered the course of Noah's ark in the midst of the deluge so His invisible hand remains at the helm of the church.

[*Chapter* 14]

To God Alone the Glory

I WAS IN AUSTIN, TEXAS, VISITING THE REGENT SCHOOL, a private elementary school modeled after the classical form of education outlined in Douglas Wilson's *Recovering the Lost Tools of Learning*. Following the direction of Dorothy Sayer's famous essay on "The Lost Tools of Learning," this school focuses on the medieval trivium: grammar, rhetoric, and dialectics. Children begin the study of Latin in the third grade.

I was speaking at a chapel service at Regent, and the schoolchildren had prepared a special treat for me. They sang the anthem *"Non nobis domine sed tua nomine da gloriam,"* which means, "Not unto us, O Lord, but unto Your name be the glory."

The words of this song hark back to Shakespeare's *Henry V,* in which the battle of Saint Crispin's Day is celebrated. When the English, being heavily outnumbered, prevailed in battle, the king ruled that no soldier was allowed to boast of the victory because all the glory belonged to God and to God alone. Henry commanded his troops to give all the glory to the providence of God.

The sentiments of the hymn are rooted in Scripture. God will share His glory with no man. The glory is never to be unto us but unto the Lord and to His name.

We remember that when God visited David with His judgment after the episode with Bathsheba, through the prophet Nathan God reminded David that he had prospered because of God's hand. We see this initially in David's stunning victory over the giant Goliath:

> And a champion went out from the camp of the Philistines, named Goliath, from Gath, whose height was six cubits and a span. He had a bronze helmet on his head, and he was armed with a coat of mail, and the weight of the coat was five thousand shekels of bronze. And he had bronze armor on his legs and a bronze javelin between his shoulders. Now the staff of his spear was like a weaver's beam, and his iron spearhead weighed six hundred shekels; and a shield-bearer went before him. Then he stood and cried out to the armies of Israel, and said to them, "Why have you come out to line up for battle? Am I not a Philistine, and you the servants of Saul? Choose a man for yourselves, and let him come down to me. If he is able to fight with me and kill me, then we will be your servants. But if I prevail against him and kill him, then you shall be our servants and serve us." (1 Sam. 17:4–9)

This challenge struck terror in the soldiers of Saul. No one stepped forward to fight against Goliath even though he repeated his challenge to the army of Israel every day for forty days, appearing each morning and each evening with the same words. Eighty times Goliath came forth, and eighty times there was no response from the cowering troops of Saul. When David visited the camp to bring provisions for his brothers he was appalled by the cowardice of the Israelites. He said:

> "What shall be done for the man who kills this Philistine and takes away the reproach from Israel? For who is this uncircumcised Philistine, that he should defy the armies of the living God?" (1 Sam. 17:26)

The soldiers explained to David that Saul had promised to enrich the warrior who would kill Goliath and give the victor his daughter in marriage and exempt his father's house from taxes. David viewed the situation as a sacred cause and volunteered his services to the king:

> Then David said to Saul, "Let no man's heart fail because of him; your servant will go and fight with this Philistine."
>
> And Saul said to David, "You are not able to go against this Philistine to fight with him; for you are a youth, and he a man of war from his youth."
>
> But David said to Saul, "Your servant used to keep his father's sheep, and when a lion or a bear came and took a lamb out of the flock, I went out after it and struck it, and delivered the lamb from its mouth; and when it arose against me, I caught it by its beard, and struck and killed it. Your servant has killed both lion and bear; and this uncircumcised Philistine will be like one of them, seeing he has defied the armies of the living God." Moreover David said, "The LORD, who delivered me from the paw of the lion and from the paw of the bear, He will deliver me from the hand of this Philistine."
>
> And Saul said to David, "Go, and the LORD be with you!" (1 Sam. 17:32–37)

David stood before King Saul, reviewing his personal history under the providence of God, and giving credit to the Lord for delivering him out of the clutches of the lion and the bear. He expressed confidence that the same Providence would deliver him from Goliath. When Saul acceded to David's request, he pronounced his blessing upon the lad and said, "The LORD be with you." David gathered smooth stones from the brook and went out against Goliath, armed only with his sling. When Goliath saw David, only a youth and wearing no armor, he was incensed by the insult:

> And when the Philistine looked about and saw David, he disdained him; for he was only a youth, ruddy and good-looking. So the Philistine said to David, "Am I a dog, that you come to me with sticks?" And the Philistine cursed David by his gods. And the

141

Philistine said to David, "Come to me, and I will give your flesh to the birds of the air and the beasts of the field!" (1 Sam. 17:42–44)

Goliath appealed to the providence of the Philistine gods, a providence that was impotent. But David was not intimidated by the giant's threats. He responded with confidence:

> "You come to me with a sword, with a spear, and with a javelin. But I come to you in the name of the Lord of hosts, the God of the armies of Israel, whom you have defied. This day the Lord will deliver you into my hand, and I will strike you and take your head from you. And this day I will give the carcasses of the camp of the Philistines to the birds of the air and the wild beasts of the earth, that all the earth may know that there is a God in Israel. Then all this assembly shall know that the Lord does not save with sword and spear; for the battle is the Lord's, and He will give you into our hands."
>
> So it was, when the Philistine arose and came and drew near to meet David, that David hastened and ran toward the army to meet the Philistine. Then David put his hand in his bag and took out a stone; and he slung it and struck the Philistine in his forehead, so that the stone sank into his forehead, and he fell on his face to the earth. So David prevailed over the Philistine with a sling and a stone, and struck the Philistine and killed him. But there was no sword in the hand of David. (1 Sam. 17:45–50)

The words of David are striking: "You come to me with a sword, with a spear, and with a javelin. But I come to you in the name of the Lord of hosts, the God of the armies of Israel, whom you have defied." Here was a clear declaration of David's utter dependence upon Providence. There was not the slightest hint of self-reliance. David declared the words that would be echoed later by Stonewall Jackson, "The battle is ours; the outcome is God's."

Clearly it was God who enabled David to accomplish the prodigious feat of slaying the giant. David had a sling in his hand, but God had David in His. The glory for the victory belonged to God.

Gideon's Handful of Warriors

Another example of a biblical hero who claimed God's providence—and then gave Him the glory came in the days of the judges, when Israel was harassed by Midianite raiders. They plundered the land, stripping the fields of the Jews and stealing their livestock. The children of Israel were forced to retreat from their homes and seek shelter in caves:

> So it was, whenever Israel had sown, Midianites would come up; also Amalekites and the people of the East would come up against them. Then they would encamp against them and destroy the produce of the earth as far as Gaza, and leave no sustenance for Israel, neither sheep nor ox nor donkey. For they would come up with their livestock and their tents, coming in as numerous as locusts; both they and their camels were without number; and they would enter the land to destroy it. So Israel was greatly impoverished because of the Midianites, and the children of Israel cried out to the LORD. (Judg. 6:3–6)

It was in these circumstances that God raised up Gideon to be a judge over Israel. While he was threshing wheat in his father's winepress (to hide it from the Midianites), an angel appeared to him and called him a "mighty man of valor." Gideon's response was one of wonderment and confusion:

> Gideon said to Him, "O my lord, if the LORD is with us, why then has all this happened to us? And where are all His miracles which our fathers told us about, saying, 'Did not the LORD bring us up from Egypt?' But now the LORD has forsaken us and delivered us into the hands of the Midianites."
>
> Then the LORD turned to him and said, "Go in this might of yours, and you shall save Israel from the hand of the Midianites. Have I not sent you?"
>
> So he said to Him, "O my Lord, how can I save Israel? Indeed my clan is the weakest in Manasseh, and I am the least in my father's house."

And the LORD said to him, "Surely I will be with you, and you shall defeat the Midianites as one man." (Judg. 6:13–16)

Gideon had some serious questions for the angel. He asked about the obvious discrepancy between the angel's promise of God's presence and the protracted suffering of the people at the hands of the Midianite marauders. He had heard of the miraculous intervention of God in the Exodus, but now, he complained, God had abandoned His people.

The angel replied with a command, a summons for Gideon to go in his might to save Israel. But Gideon, not perceiving himself to be a mighty man of valor, stumbled at the command and the promise of victory. He protested that his clan was the weakest in Manasseh and that he was the weakest in his own family. To assure Gideon that the God of the Exodus was not dead and still had the power to perform miracles, the angel performed a miracle for Gideon right on the spot:

> The Angel of God said to him, "Take the meat and the unleavened bread and lay them on this rock, and pour out the broth." And he did so.
>
> Then the Angel of the LORD put out the end of the staff that was in His hand, and touched the meat and the unleavened bread; and fire rose out of the rock and consumed the meat and the unleavened bread. And the Angel of the LORD departed out of his sight.
>
> Now Gideon perceived that He was the Angel of the LORD. So Gideon said, "Alas, O Lord GOD! For I have seen the Angel of the LORD face to face."
>
> Then the LORD said to him, "Peace be with you; do not fear, you shall not die." (Judg. 6:20–23)

Notice that the mysterious angel is called the "Angel of God" but Gideon responded to the angel as if He were the presence of God Himself, giving rise to the speculation that the appearance of the angel was a preincarnation manifestation of Christ, a "Christophany."

Gideon continued to test God with the incident of the fleece (see Judges 6:36–40) to gain assurance that God's promise would indeed come to pass. When he was finally convinced, Gideon amassed a huge army of over thirty thousand troops to go up against the Midianites. But God intervened and began to cull the army, paring it down to a smaller and smaller number. He explained His reasons to Gideon:

> "The people who are with you are too many for Me to give the Midianites into their hands, lest Israel claim glory for itself against Me, saying, 'My own hand has saved me.' Now therefore, proclaim in the hearing of the people, saying, 'Whoever is fearful and afraid, let him turn and depart at once from Mount Gilead.'" And twenty-two thousand of the people returned, and ten thousand remained.
>
> But the LORD said to Gideon, "The people are still too many; bring them down to the water, and I will test them for you there. Then it will be, that of whom I say to you, 'This one shall go with you,' the same shall go with you; and of whomever I say to you, 'This one shall not go with you,' the same shall not go." So he brought the people down to the water. And the LORD said to Gideon, "Everyone who laps from the water with his tongue, as a dog laps, you shall set apart by himself; likewise everyone who gets down on his knees to drink." And the number of those who lapped, putting their hand to their mouth, was three hundred men; but all the rest of the people got down on their knees to drink water. (Judg. 7:2–6)

God was preparing His people to sing the *non nobis domine*. He reduced the army from thirty-two thousand men to three hundred men so Israel would not claim glory for itself. The biblical axiom that salvation was of the Lord was to stay intact.

Then God commanded Gideon to go with his servant into the camp of the Midianite army at night to spy out the situation. In the darkness Gideon overheard one of the Midianite soldiers tell of a dream he had had that gave a foreboding sign that Midian would be defeated by Gideon. When Gideon heard this, he immediately worshiped God, then he returned to his own men and announced to them that for all intents and purposes the battle was already won:

> "When I blow the trumpet, I and all who are with me, then you also blow the trumpets on every side of the whole camp, and say, 'The sword of the LORD and of Gideon!'"
> So Gideon and the hundred men who were with him came to the outpost of the camp at the beginning of the middle watch, just as they had posted the watch; and they blew the trumpets and broke the pitchers that were in their hands. Then the three companies blew the trumpets and broke the pitchers—they held the torches in their left hands and the trumpets in their right hands for blowing—and they cried, "The sword of the LORD and of Gideon!" And every man stood in his place all around the camp; and the whole army ran and cried out and fled. When the three hundred blew the trumpets, the LORD set every man's sword against his companion throughout the whole camp; and the army fled to Beth Acacia, toward Zererah, as far as the border of Abel Meholah, by Tabbath. (Judg. 7:18–22)

The victory came through a cleverly devised ruse. Gideon's three hundred men made such a racket they gave the impression of an attacking horde. The Midianites were thrown into panic and fled for the borders. In their confusion, the Midianites even slaughtered each other. In the melee 120,000 Midian soldiers were killed.

Then many of the men of Israel, instead of celebrating this fabulous feat, began complaining that they had not been included in the victory. They were like those, of whom King Henry spoke, who were in their beds on the day of the great Saint Crispin's Day victory.

God and the Exodus

The glory for this victory belonged to the God of providence. God had orchestrated the battle in such a way that the odds so heavily favored the enemy, the only way victory could come was by divine intervention. This was not the first nor the last time God did this sort of thing to ensure that the people would not miss His providential hand. In the Exodus itself God declared that it was He who would effect the redemption of the nation:

"Therefore say to the children of Israel: I am the LORD; I will bring you out from under the burdens of the Egyptians, I will rescue you from their bondage, and I will redeem you with an outstretched arm and with great judgments. I will take you as My people, and I will be your God. Then you shall know that I am the LORD your God who brings you out from under the burdens of the Egyptians. And I will bring you into the land which I swore to give to Abraham, Isaac, and Jacob; and I will give it to you as a heritage: I am the LORD.'" (Exod. 6:6–8)

The events of the Exodus, including the plagues and God's hardening the heart of Pharaoh, were designed to make it clear to the Egyptians and to the Israelites that it was God who would bring the Exodus to pass:

"And I will harden Pharaoh's heart, and multiply My signs and My wonders in the land of Egypt. But Pharaoh will not heed you, so that I may lay My hand on Egypt and bring My armies and My people, the children of Israel, out of the land of Egypt by great judgments. And the Egyptians shall know that I am the LORD, when I stretch out My hand on Egypt and bring out the children of Israel from among them." (Exod. 7:3–5)

In all of these events, all of these victories against all odds, the people of God were being taught to sing the *non nobis domine.* The glory belongs to the majesty of God and to His name and His name alone.

Chapter 15

Train Wreck

I WAS RIDING ON A BUS WITH MY WIFE IN MOBILE, Alabama. We were seated on a bench at the front of the bus. Across from us on the opposite bench were three people, a young man and his wife and the young man's mother. The young woman was obviously in distress; her hair was wet and stringy, and she had wrapped a blanket around herself. Her lips were blue, and her teeth were chattering. As I watched her shiver I noticed that she had neither socks nor shoes on her feet. This was not the usual sight one sees on a bus!

I wanted to help this young woman, but I wasn't quite sure what I could do for her. I removed my shoes and my socks and then handed my socks to her. My shoes were of no use to her as they were too big for her tiny feet. She smiled and thanked me as she donned my socks and doubled them over to provide more insulation from the cold. When the bus reached its destination we all got off, and I never saw the young woman—or the socks—again. I wonder what she did with them . . .

Though I never saw these people again I did read about them the very next day on the front page of *USA Today*. The newspaper article recounted the same story the couple had related to us aboard the bus, an incredible story of survival. The destination of the bus we had ridden together was a hospital, ironically named Providence Hospital. We were taken to this hospital because we had just been in the worst train wreck in the history of Amtrak, the crash of the *Sunset Limited,* which had plunged into the waters of an Alabama bayou. This wreck killed more people than have been killed in all the other train wrecks in Amtrak's history combined.

The couple and the woman they were with were the only survivors from one of the coaches that had plunged into the water and was submerged at the bottom of the bayou. The husband told me that when the accident occurred he had had five seconds to push out the emergency window and pull his wife and mother out of the train and into the murky water. Holding hands, they had struggled to reach the surface. When they broke through and their lungs gasped for air, they flailed with their feet and arms as they fought to tread water. The husband said he was surprised to find something solid under his feet. He later realized he was standing on the roof of the submerged coach. Together they made their way to shore and to safety, escaping both the water and the flames that were roiling around them.

My wife and I had boarded that train in New Orleans. It was behind schedule, running a couple of hours late, and we boarded sometime after midnight. Our sleeping compartment was already made up; the steward led us to our room, where we retired immediately. At three o'clock in the morning I was awakened while flying through the air in the darkness of our cabin. I heard the screeching sound of metal against metal as the train car bounced to a halt. I was experiencing the law of inertia. The train was stopping suddenly, but I continued moving until I crashed into the opposite compartment wall. The first words I heard were from my wife, asking me if I was hurt. I said I was okay and asked her the same question. She said she was uninjured. Then the steward was at our door, asking if we were hurt. The woman in the next compartment was screaming that she was bleeding and she couldn't open her door. As I moved to open our door so I could help the steward get to the woman, I fumbled with the lock and couldn't get it open. With quiet calm, my wife reached over in the darkness and opened it for me.

In the initial moments of the crash I was not alarmed. Perhaps it was shock. I assumed the train had been involved in an accident with an automobile, an event that is all too commonplace at railroad crossings. But when I stepped into the corridor to help the steward get the woman's door open, I saw something that changed my initial assessment. A huge column of fire rose fifty to seventy-five feet into the air forward and right of our car. Now I assumed we had hit a gasoline truck to create such a fire. My wife had not yet seen the flames, so I (trying to sound calm) said to her, "Vesta, we need to get off the train." She said she had to find her clothes and her shoes before she would get off. She quickly got dressed and handed me my clothes so I could dress quickly as well. I could see that the flames were moving in our direction and again advised Vesta to hurry up and get off the train. She would have none of it. She wasn't getting off until she found our shoes. I said, "Forget the shoes. We need to get off *now!*"

She found our shoes, and we finally went down the stairs and got off the train fully clothed. We were the last ones off. A train worker helped us off and herded us to the rear of the train and down the tracks, away from the fire. Vesta had no injuries. She had been asleep in the upper berth when the accident occurred, and her inertia was arrested by a leather harness designed to keep passengers in the upper berth from rolling out of bed in the night. The lower berths have no harnesses.

From our vantage point at the rear of the train, the scene before us was almost surrealistic. Dense fog mixed with clouds of smoke rose from the swamp. The pillar of flames was still visible on the right side of the train. I could see the ray of a boat's searchlight eerily piercing the fog and smoke, and I could make out the form of train cars protruding from the water at a strange angle. I had no idea that more cars were submerged beneath them. Scores of people were milling around by the tracks, many with blankets. I don't know how many people had survived the water, but it was certainly more than fifty. None of us realized the full gravity of the moment. There were no shrieks of pain or panic among the survivors. There was no realization that so many people had been killed. Those who perished died in the first minutes after the crash, entrapped in the submerged cars.

As the danger of the fire passed, I moved back toward the train and noticed that our car was resting on a bridge, its wheels off the track. Ours had been the last car on the train. I went back on the train to retrieve our luggage. With my eyes adjusting to the darkness and by the glimmer of light from the glow of the fire, I could tell our room was in shambles.

After I got off the train again and rejoined my wife, we sat by the tracks with the rest of the survivors for three hours waiting for help to come. A helicopter arrived and hovered above the wreck with a searchlight peering down at us. The accident had occurred in such a remote area there was no access to it via car or truck. The only access for the rescue workers was by train, and at this point there was only one track to use in either direction. We later learned that a freight train was behind us and when the accident was reported to it via radio, it had to stop and back up an hour's journey to Mobile to get clear of the track so a rescue train could come to the site.

When the rescue train arrived it had three coaches filled with firemen, paramedics, and policemen. A quick triage was conducted, and the survivors were put aboard the three coaches according to the severity of their injuries. Those in the greatest distress boarded the nearest car; Vesta and I proceeded to the furthest car. Like the freight train, the rescue train had to go backward toward Mobile. During that hour-long trip two passengers on our car suffered heart attacks. When the train reached the outskirts of Mobile at a major highway intersection, we got off the train and were processed through another triage point. More than one hundred ambulances were assembled there, some of them coming from as far away as Florida to help in the rescue.

That's when we boarded the bus for Providence Hospital, a trip that took almost an hour. We were amazed at the masses of people that lined the expressway and followed the progress of our bus as it was led by two police motorcycles to the hospital. When we arrived at Providence Hospital about one hundred hospital people were waiting at the front entrance to treat those of us on the bus. My wife and I were checked over by physicians and then released. I seemed to have no injuries and was simply eager to get out of there and call home. I didn't realize I had sustained a back injury until the next day.

We were not able to get to a telephone until more than five hours after the accident. We weren't all that concerned, however, because we assumed that no one in Orlando would have heard of the accident. Eventually I called our office, and when the receptionist answered and recognized my voice she started to cry. Footage from the crash site had already aired on CNN, and our friends and family did not know if we were living or dead. My staff told me my son and one of my close associates were already at the airport ready to board a plane for Mobile. I told my secretary to call the airport and have them paged so they would know we were all right.

We left Providence Hospital in the care of one of their administrators, who kindly drove us to the airport. At the airport we saw people gathered around a television set that was showing footage from the accident scene. Now the sun had risen, and the view was clear. It was then, from listening to the news report on television, that we first learned of the full magnitude of the accident. It was a weird experience, standing there watching the story we had just lived through unfold on television.

What actually happened in that Alabama bayou? The later investigations put all the pieces together. It began with the problem of the fog, which caused a commercial boat pushing barges across the water to become disoriented. Inadvertently it began to travel up the mouth of the waterway, which was closed to boat traffic. To make matters worse, one of the heavy steel barges suddenly broke loose from the boat and became a runaway in the water, crashing into the railroad bridge. But this bridge was not a normal drawbridge. It was built originally as a swivel bridge that pivoted open to allow boats to pass. When the waterway was closed to boat traffic, the swivel point was welded shut in the closed position. When the runaway barge hit the bridge, it hit it precisely at the swivel point, breaking the weld and moving the bridge open just enough to separate the train rails.

Now, Amtrak has a warning system built into its rails. When a track separates, an electric current is disrupted, which then signals the train that a track is separated ahead. But the separation occurred only seconds before the train reached the bridge, so the engineer had no time to stop or even slow down. The brand-new supercharged engine literally flew off the bridge and plunged into the muck of the bayou, burying itself and its crew in the ground more than eighty feet below the bridge. When the engine left the bridge, the fuel lines were broken, spilling tons of diesel fuel into the water, which ignited into a tower of flame. As more cars rolled off the bridge and into the water, the momentum of the back cars was slowed as the cars fell on top of each other in accordion fashion. All of this happened in seconds as a result of a "freak" combination of events that culminated in the crash.

Some "good" things also happened during this sequence of events that helped many people survive. The configuration of the pileup of cars forced some cars to land on the left side of the bridge, away from the blazing inferno. Many more passengers would surely have been killed if all the cars had fallen into the flames.

When we arrived home in Orlando, we had just entered our front door and set down our luggage in the foyer when the doorbell rang. We turned to answer the door and found a camera crew from the television station and a group of people pointing microphones at us. The reporters asked all kinds of questions, like, "Why do you think this happened?" "Why do you think your life was spared?" "What did you learn theologically from this tragedy?" I told the newsmen I had no earthly idea why the accident happened. I also told them I had no idea why we were spared and that I hadn't learned anything theologically from the wreck that I didn't already know. I said we had certainly experienced afresh the tender mercy of God and were profoundly grateful for His providential care. That doesn't mean the survivors were better off than those who perished. Surely some of those who died that morning were ushered into glory and were far better off than we were at that moment!

No Room for Fate

I knew that on the horizontal plane of history this train wreck was a horrible tragedy. I also knew that on the vertical plane there are no accidents. I understood that the invisible hand of Providence was involved in this "accident," and it was one of those events that work together for good for those who love the Lord.

When we consider all the things that combined to create the train wreck, we may be tempted to think it was caused by a weird combination of chance events. On a human level we consider the 1993 wreck of the *Sunset Limited* an accident. It *was* an accident in the sense that the boat captain did not intend to ram the bridge with his barge and the locomotive engineer did not intentionally run the train off the bridge.

In contrast the *Sunset Limited* had another wreck in 1995, this time on a trestle near Phoenix, Arizona. That wreck resulted in one fatality and scores of injuries. The preliminary reports indicated that this wreck was not an accident but an intentional act of sabotage. As Providence would have it, I missed that wreck, but not by much. That train had originated in Miami on its way to Los Angeles. I had boarded that same train in Fort Lauderdale but got off in Orlando, long before the wreck occurred. But many of my fellow passengers were involved in it.

Often the language of the reporters when they comment on such accidents includes references to the "ill-fated train," or the "ill-fated plane." I hope this is merely a manner of speaking and that the reporters do not really believe that the destiny of human beings is in the hands of "fate." The fates were part of the mythological system of the ancient world, and they were depicted as arbitrary, capricious, and mischievous sub-deities who wreaked havoc among people. Today fate is sometimes seen as a blind force of nature that causes horrible things or good things to happen to us.

The doctrine of the providence of God leaves no room for fate, blind or otherwise. God is not blind; neither is He capricious. For Him there are no accidents. With God there are no cases of chance events. As I have labored to demonstrate in my book *Not a Chance,* there is no such thing as chance. The word *chance* is a meaningful term to describe mathematical possibilities. We can calculate the odds of various things happening given certain conditions. But chance itself does not contribute to the event. It does not *cause* anything.

Chance does not cause anything to happen because it has no power to do anything. It has no power to do anything because chance itself is not a thing that exercises power or force. It is not a thing; it has no being. And since it has no being, it can exert no force. *Chance* is a word, not a power. For something to exercise force it must have being or it can have no force. It is still an axiom of both philosophy and science that *ex nihilo, nihil fit,* out of nothing, nothing comes. Nothing cannot do something. Since chance is nothing, it cannot do anything.

Yet we speak of "chance events," not because the events have no cause, but because we either did not intend to cause the actual results that occurred or because we don't know what the actual causes of the events are. In this case the word *chance* functions as a substitute for the word *ignorance.*

Consider the plague that afflicted the Philistines when they held the ark of God in captivity and the Philistine sages wondered if there was a causal connection between the presence of the ark and the presence of the plague. They devised an elaborate plan to decide the matter:

> "Now therefore, make a new cart, take two milk cows which have
> never been yoked, and hitch the cows to the cart; and take their

calves home, away from them. Then take the ark of the LORD and set it on the cart; and put the articles of gold which you are returning to Him as a trespass offering in a chest by its side. Then send it away, and let it go. And watch: if it goes up the road to its own territory, to Beth Shemesh, then He has done us this great evil. But if not, then we shall know that it is not His hand that struck us—it happened to us by chance." (1 Sam. 6:7–9)

Though the Philistines were religious people, having a temple to the god Dagon, this experiment indicated a certain ignorance and superstition among them. If they really believed the plague occurred "by chance" then they were not theists at all. If chance exists, God cannot exist. If one molecule flies wild by chance, then God is not sovereign. If God is not sovereign, then God is not God. God and chance simply cannot coexist.

Perhaps the Philistine sages were simply speaking in a figurative sense. Maybe what they really meant to say was that either the plague was caused by God or by something else. Perhaps it was a mere coincidence that the plague occurred at the same time as the ark of God was being held captive. It could have been an expression describing ignorance of other possible causes that were unknown to them. I will grant them that much. But if they really believed that chance could actually cause a plague or anything else, then they were talking nonsense.

Unfortunately such manner of speaking continues to this day, and learned people, including theologians, philosophers, and scientists, sometimes speak of chance as if it actually had some power. This is a reversion to superstition and a departure from serious science or philosophy. If we push the question to the ultimate level and ask the question, "What are the chances that things happen by chance?" the only appropriate answer we can give is, "Not a chance."

Accidents are events we do not intend to take place. But there is another intentionality that transcends our intentionality. The intentions of God, as seen in the concurrence between the intents of Joseph's brothers and the intent of God, are never subject to chance or fate. Chance is a repugnant term to ascribe to the actions of God. Albert Einstein was correct when he said, "God doesn't roll dice."

Chapter 16

Providence and the Problem of Evil

THE PROBLEM OF EVIL HAS BEEN CALLED THE "ACHILLES heel" of Christianity. It is perhaps the most vexing philosophical issue we face when we consider the full magnitude of the providence of God. The question is as simple as the answer is difficult: How can a God who is absolutely good allow evil in His creation? It is a question of *theodicy*, or the justification of God, for the presence of an imperfect universe.

John Stuart Mill, among others, argued that, given the presence of evil in the world, God is either not omnipotent or not loving (or good). If evil exists because God does not want it to exist but is unable to prevent it, then He is not omnipotent. If He is omnipotent but allows it to exist, then He is neither loving nor good. Either way the presence of evil is fatal to Christianity, according to Mill.

In theology evil is referred to as "the mystery of inequity." Christianity clearly admits that evil exists. Indeed, most religions admit to its existence, with the exception of those few that argue that evil is an illusion. Christian Science, for example, holds this belief. I once had a debate with a Christian Scientist on this point. I maintained that evil was real, and he insisted that it was an illusion.

I asked him if he thought I was an illusion. He allowed that I was real. I asked him if he thought my view of evil was correct. He said it was not. Then I asked him if he thought it was a good thing that I was teaching people that evil really exists. He said "No." I then asked him if my teaching about evil was evil. He saw the trap but didn't slow down. He said that my teaching about evil was an illusion. I guess that meant my teaching that evil was real was not real teaching or that my evil teaching about evil only seemed to be evil but in reality was good, which would mean that evil really exists. The debate gave me a headache, or at least the illusion of a headache.

The philosopher Leibniz provided a famous "theodicy" in which he concluded that God has created the best of all possible worlds. Leibniz did not come glibly to his conclusion that this is the best of all possible worlds. He took several factors into consideration. First, he considered that God could have chosen from several possible models when He undertook to create a world. Whatever model He finally chose would have been chosen according to His infinite wisdom, omniscience, and righteousness. Any other "possible" model would have been rejected. We might conceive of a better world than the one that is, but we lack the eternal perspective necessary to make the final kind of judgment God is able to make. God alone thinks *sub species aeternitatis,* or under the auspices of the eternal.

Second, Leibniz argued that only God is perfect and it is impossible for God to create another God. The second God would not really be God because by definition anything that God creates must be a creature. It would be a dependent, derived, and contingent being, not God. The concept of omnipotence does not mean that God can do anything, only that He has complete power and control over what He does create.

There was something else lurking in Leibniz's thought that was critical to his theory. He made a distinction among three types of evil: *moral* evil, *physical* evil, and *metaphysical* evil. Moral evil has to do with the sin of volitional creatures. Physical evil refers to sickness or natural calamities such as earthquakes and floods. Both moral and physical evil flow out of and are a result of what Leibniz called metaphysical evil, which has to do with imperfect being. Basically it is related to finitude. Anything that is created, or is finite, is a lower order of being than the pure eternal and infinite being found in God. Since the finite being is a lower form of being than an infinite being, it is metaphysically impure, or "evil." It lacks the perfection of a being found in God alone. Medieval theologians were fond of referring to God as *ens perfectissimum*, or the "most perfect being."

For Christians, the problem with this schema is that it makes sin a necessary consequence of creation, or of finitude. This flies in the face of the biblical prohibition of sin and the biblical promise of God's judgment against it. If moral evil is a necessary consequence of metaphysical evil, then the question of culpability is raised.

The biblical record of creation does not say either man or the cosmos created evil. Rather, the divine evaluation of the work of creation is that it was good. The fall was a fall from original righteousness and is not viewed biblically as a necessary consequence of creation.

Many other attempts of theodicy have been made. One of the most common is the philosophy of *dualism*, which maintains the eternal coexistence of forces of good and evil. This view has been prominent in various Eastern philosophies and religions. It sees two equal and opposite forces locked in an eternal cosmic struggle. It is light versus darkness, ying and yang, etc. This type of thinking often invades Christian thought when Satan is regarded as an evil being who is equal in power and eternity with God.

Dualism is also fatal to Christianity as it makes redemption an inherent impossibility. If the two forces are equal and opposite from all eternity, there is no hope of either ever emerging triumphant. Also, it is the death of Christian theology because God is no longer ultimate. It is the end of monotheism as well because dualism posits the existence of at least two distinct deities.

In recent times some process theologians have placed the poles of good and evil into the nature of God Himself; God vacillates between the two poles, they say. God becomes like the Roman god Janus, adorned with two faces. God is no longer deemed absolutely holy but contains a shadow side to His character from which comes evil.

Unfortunately, most theodicies that seek to explain the origin of evil raise more questions than they answer and leave us with more theological problems than the problem of evil. It is a case of the cure being worse than the disease.

The Nature of Evil

The problem of evil must be addressed first by asking questions about the nature of evil. The Westminster Catechism answers the question, "What is sin?" by the answer, "Sin is any want of conformity to or transgression of the law of God." The answer contains an important negative term, the word *want*. A want is a lack or deficiency of something. This word was carefully chosen by the framers of the catechism to conform to classic definitions of evil. Both Augustine and Thomas Aquinas defined evil in terms of negation or privation (*negatio* and *privatio*), referring to the lack, or privation, of something, namely the good. Evil is a lack of goodness, the negation of goodness.

The theologians understood that evil is characteristically defined in negative terms. We speak of *unrighteousness, injustice, lawlessness,* or *antichrist*. Sin is described as *disobedience*. We cannot understand unrighteousness except against the standard of righteousness. Likewise, injustice is defined by contrasting it to justice and disobedience by contrasting it to obedience. It has been said that evil is parasitic; it cannot exist except as a privation or negation of the good. Augustine argued that evil depends upon the good for its very definition.

Because evil is defined in such negative terms it may be tempting to say that if evil is negation, or if privation cannot be absolute, then perhaps evil doesn't really exist after all. We cannot conceive of pure nothingness. If something were absolutely evil it would be an absolute negation, which would be nothing. Or if it were pure privation it would likewise be nothing. We can think of absolute goodness but not absolute evil.

To protect against the conclusion that evil doesn't exist, the magisterial Reformers of the sixteenth century added a descriptive word to the classical definition of evil by calling evil *privatio actuosa*. They agreed that evil is a kind of privation but is nevertheless real. It is both actual and *active*. Evil is something that moral agents *do*. This "doing" may be either active or passive. It may involve sins of commission or sins of omission. A sin of omission is a failure to do what we ought to do. But even this "not doing" is a certain kind of doing because it involves doing something other than what we should do.

Augustine insisted that sin or evil is something that only a good creature can actually do. That is, the creature must first be good before it is capable of doing bad. He argued that Adam was created good but not immutably good. He had the ability to sin (*posse peccare*) and the ability to not sin (*posse non peccare*). That he exercised his ability to sin is a matter of record. Part of what Augustine was getting at is that since evil is a lack of good it depends upon the good for its very existence.

Perhaps the only comfort we can draw from this is that those who complain that evil is a problem can only do so once they have affirmed the existence of the good. If we are unable to account for the origin of evil, the critic has a double problem. If he insists that evil is real, then he must also affirm the existence of good. If there is no God, he is left, not only with accounting for evil, but for the good as well.

This is the dilemma that leads many skeptics to conclude that evil really doesn't exist after all. But then neither does good. This view reduces to nihilism and the idea that we live in an amoral universe: There is neither good nor evil, only conventions and preferences. This view is integrally related to a relativistic view of life. Relativism insists that there are no absolutes except the absolute that there are absolutely no absolutes. In this philosophy all things are permissible.

I once was visited by a distraught Christian woman who complained to me that her son was a professed atheist. She begged me to talk with him, and I agreed to do it, knowing in advance that the son would probably resent the meeting. He came, openly hostile and obviously reluctant to be there. I asked him how he felt about his mother's views. He complained bitterly that his mother was always trying to shove her religion down his throat. I asked him why he didn't like that. He said he believed everybody should have the right to do his or her own thing. Then I asked him why then he would complain about his mother's behavior. Didn't she also have the right to do her own thing? I explained that his mother, being a professed Christian, was called to be sensitive to him and not coercive in her behavior. From a Christian perspective, he had some just grounds for his complaint, but according to his "ethic" he had no grounds whatsoever. He got the point.

Most relativists are only relatively relativists. That is, they want to express their own rights of preference and will tolerate other people's preferences—until they bump up against their own. This is why Kant argued that the existence of God was a practical necessity for the survival of civilization. Without some norms to govern human behavior, we are left with moral anarchy, a situation in which society cannot survive for long.

All cultures have norms. Perhaps the norms are simply conventions or the preferences of the controlling powers. If that is the case and the preferences are not universally held, then manifestly somebody is being tyrannized. Nietzsche argued that these norms are mere conventions people follow in a "herd morality" because they are not bright enough or courageous enough to challenge them.

However, we must admit that practical necessity is not an adequate proof for the reality of God. Perhaps the nihilist is right. There is no God. Nothing is either right or wrong, and we live in a cosmic jungle. I don't believe that. I am convinced that sound and compelling argument can be given for the existence of God and of good and evil. But at least I admire the pure nihilist for not copping out to silly alternatives like the humanists do, wanting to have their cake and eat it too. The humanist exalts the dignity of man and the importance of various virtues while at the same time declaring that we are cosmic accidents. Slime has no virtue, and the humanist can give no compelling reason why any human being should have any rights because he has no justifying grounds for rights in the first place. He has only sentiment, which proves nothing except the emotional state of the avower.

No Easy Answers

Frequently I hear Christians give an easy answer to the problem of evil; they declare facilely that evil originates in man's free will. I call this a facile answer because it fails to get to the root of the problem. It is plain, from Scripture, that man chose evil instead of good in the Garden of Eden. But it doesn't explain how a creature that was created good chose evil. Let us look at the biblical account of the fall:

> Now the serpent was more cunning than any beast of the field which the LORD God had made. And he said to the woman, "Has God indeed said, 'You shall not eat of every tree of the garden'?"
>
> And the woman said to the serpent, "We may eat the fruit of the trees of the garden; but of the fruit of the tree which is in the midst of the garden, God has said, 'You shall not eat it, nor shall you touch it, lest you die.'"
>
> Then the serpent said to the woman, "You will not surely die. For God knows that in the day you eat of it your eyes will be opened, and you will be like God, knowing good and evil."
>
> So when the woman saw that the tree was good for food, that it was pleasant to the eyes, and a tree desirable to make one wise, she took of its fruit and ate. She also gave to her husband with her, and

he ate. Then the eyes of both of them were opened, and they knew that they were naked; and they sewed fig leaves together and made themselves coverings. (Gen. 3:1–7)

The text indicates that Adam and Eve chose to do something God had commanded them not to do. Their doing it proves with certainty that they were able to do it. The question is, *Why* did they do it? And *how* were they able to do it? Various explanations are given. The first is that the serpent coerced them to do it ("the devil made them do it" excuse). This explanation has two serious problems. The first is that the Scripture gives no indication that they were victims of coercion. The second is that if they were forced into the act the guilt would be Satan's and not theirs. They could not justly be held responsible for doing something they were forced to do by Satan.

The second explanation is that they were deceived by Satan. The Scriptures do indicate that Satan is subtle, crafty, beguiling, and is capable of being highly deceptive. Indeed, he is the Great Deceiver. The problem with this explanation, however, is the assigning of guilt to innocent victims of deception. If Adam and Eve were totally deceived they would have sinned in ignorance. Certainly deception occurred. Satan told them that by eating the forbidden fruit they would be as gods and that they would not die. Both of these assertions were lies. They ate and did not become as God. They ate, and they did die.

It is also clear from the text that Adam and Eve could not claim ignorance as an excuse. They were told and told clearly what God commanded and what He forbade. They acted in the clear knowledge of these things and could not say they were totally deceived.

So the question comes back to free will. We grant that Adam and Eve freely willed to sin, but the deeper question remains: Why? Obviously they sinned because they wanted to sin. They had a desire to sin. But the desire to sin is already sin. They committed an evil action out of an evil desire. Without the desire they could not sin. If they acted against their desire then they would be acting against their own will, and the choice would not have been a free choice. If the act was truly free and they acted according to their desire then they must have had an evil desire or inclination to start with. From whence did it come? Was it there from the beginning? Did God give them the evil desire? If He did, how could He hold them culpable? If He didn't give it to them, where did it come from?

These are no small questions allowing easy answers. This dilemma provoked Karl Barth to describe the origin of sin as an "impossible possibility." These words are, of course, an oxymoron, a veritable nonsense statement. If it were impossible, then it couldn't have been a possibility. If it was a possibility, then it couldn't have been impossible. The use of the oxymoron does not resolve the problem; it only underlines the dilemma.

I do not know the solution to the problem of evil. Nor do I know of anyone else who does. I have never been fully satisfied by any of the theodicies I've ever seen. This does not mean the problem is insoluble or that the question is unanswerable. Perhaps tomorrow the problem will be solved. But so far I haven't been able to find a solution. My ability to identify the problem is no solution to the problem. Diagnosis or analysis is not a cure.

This does not mean I have not reached any conclusions on the matter. I have concluded that evil is real. I also agree that evil is dependent on the good for its very definition and that evil must be defined in terms of privation and negation. Most importantly perhaps is the conclusion that ultimately it must be good that there is evil or evil would not exist.

We must be exceedingly careful here. To say it is good that evil exists is not the same thing as saying that evil is good. To say evil is good is itself is evil, as Scripture so clearly declares. Evil is evil. However, to say that it is good that there is evil is simply to declare that God is good and that His providence extends to all things, including evil. God's sovereignty stands over evil, and He is able to bring good out of evil and to use evil for His holy purposes. When I say it is good that there is evil I'm saying that evil could not exist for a second apart from the providence of God. That God allows, permits, or ordains that there be evil means He deems it good to allow it. He only ordains what He wills should take place. His will is perfectly and absolutely righteous. If He wills that evil should exist and it could not possibly exist if He did not will it, then we must conclude that in His secret counsel He has good reasons that evil should exist. The only reasons He has for anything are good reasons. He wills whatsoever He wills according to His good pleasure. There is no bad pleasure to be found in Him or in His will. Evil is real, and it is evil. But evil is proximate, not ultimate. It is not the final answer of God who works all things according to His inscrutable but righteous will.

Evil is a problem to Christianity, but it is not fatal to Christianity. In all things we must interpret the unknown in light of the known, not the known in light of the unknown. What is known is that God exists and that He is good. What is also known is that we sin and that only God can solve that problem and that He has solved it for us in Christ. We also know that sin is not a necessary consequence of finitude because in heaven we will still be finite and we will not sin. There we will enjoy the best of all possible heavens.

Chapter 17

All Things Work for Good

WE HAVE SEEN THAT IT IS EVIL TO CALL EVIL GOOD OR GOOD evil. This judgment is designed to avoid confusing the two. Yet, by distinguishing between that which is proximate, or immediate, and that which is ultimate, or remote, we can say that it is good that there is evil. What are the implications of this?

We frequently present seminars on the subject of the providence of God. During these seminars I ask the audience how they would feel if Christ walked into the room and announced that from this moment forward nothing bad would ever happen to us. Everyone is quick to say they would feel an enormous sense of relief.

Such an announcement from Christ would go a long way to free us from the assault of anxiety. Fear and worry are two dimensions of life that affect us all. Besides making us uncomfortable, they leave scars from stress on both our bodies and our souls. Yes, life without fear or worry would be a sheer delight.

It is significant that the negative command, or prohibition, that Jesus most frequently uttered was "Fear not." I have often wondered why this was so. Jesus said the words "fear not" so often that it almost seems like it was a customary form of greeting in the ancient world. Of course it was not, but the customary greeting

"Shalom" or "Peace" was not far removed from the words "Fear not."

When I leave the dentist's office after a series of visits and know that I don't have to return for six months, I feel a temporary euphoria. I am free from one worry for a season. But worry has a way of reappearing like the mythical multiheaded monster. Cut off one head of the Hydra, and she grows another in its place. The essence of fear and worry is that something bad will happen to us, that we will suffer from some sort of physical evil such as disease, injury, accident, loss of property or finances, etc., or we will suffer as the result of someone's act of moral evil against us or from the consequences of our own acts.

All Things Work for Good

To live in an environment where there is no evil of any kind, either physical or moral, would be literally "heaven." But at the present time we live on earth, not in heaven. We are still in the vale of tears, and we walk through the valley of death; we walk in this valley fearing evil despite the courage of the psalmist. David could say that he feared no evil because he could also say that God was with him. It was the assurance of God's presence that dispelled his fear. Behind Jesus' command "Fear not" was the clear reason for the exile of fear, "For I am with you."

But we do not see Jesus with our eyes or hear His voice with our ears. He has not walked visibly into our church buildings and announced that from this day forth no evil will befall us. Yet in another sense He has done precisely that. In and through the apostolic word we have the promise of Christ that no evil will befall us. How so? To answer this we must turn our attention to one of the most well-known and comforting texts of the New Testament:

> And we know that all things work together for good to those who love God, to those who are the called according to His purpose. (Rom. 8:28)

We note that Paul does not say here that all things that happen to us are good things. In fact, bad things happen to us. Painful things. Things that crush our spirits. Things that leave wounds and scars. Things that evoke grief and lead us into the house of mourning. Yet all of these bad things that happen to us are working together for our good. This is to say that ultimately it is good that these things happen to us.

Four Categories of Reality

Again we stress the importance of not confusing good and evil. We have said that it is evil to call good evil or evil good. This involves moral dishonesty. But if we fix our attention on the distinction between the proximate and the remote we gain a different perspective.

Dr. John Gerstner has frequently distinguished four categories of reality. They include:

- good good
- bad good
- bad bad
- good bad

At first glance these categories seem to represent an exercise in oxymoronism. But let us give them the benefit of a second glance.

Good Good

Good good is good in the ultimate sense. It is goodness as conceived in the full biblical sense; the Bible says no one does good (see Romans 3). Yet from another perspective people are said to do good things. Jesus rebuked the rich young ruler for calling Him good because the man said this without knowing to whom he was speaking. Indeed Jesus was good, and the good He did was good good. For a deed to be considered good in the sight of God, it must meet two qualifications. The first is that it must conform outwardly to the law of God. The second is that it must be motivated internally by a genuine love for God. The Great Commandment requires that we love God with our whole heart. Such unmixed love, an absolutely pure love, is not found perfectly in the hearts of fallen creatures. This is what prompted Augustine to regard our good works as being at best "splendid vices." If we conform outwardly to the law of God yet do so with motives that lack a perfect love for God, this lack mars the perfection of the work. Good good, then, is good that not only perfectly fulfills the outward law of God but proceeds from a perfect internal love for God.

Bad Good

Bad good is that good that outwardly conforms to the law of God but is motivated by impure motives. Calvin, for example, allowed that pagans are able to perform acts of what he called "civil virtue"—works of charity or of righteousness that are strictly external. A pagan sometimes drives his car within the legal speed limit. He does this not because he has a deep desire to honor God and show his love for Him by obeying the civil magistrates God has ordained. He has his own reasons for obeying the speed limit. He may be trying to avoid a ticket, or he may simply enjoy driving at that particular speed. He may be acting out of what Jonathan Edwards called an "enlightened self-interest." His interest, or motive, is self-centered rather than God-centered. We even see this pound of flesh present in the "good" works of believers.

Bad Bad

Bad bad, or evil evil, may be defined as evil or badness that has no salutary aspect to it. It is unmitigated evil. It is evil in the full and final sense. The sin that the impenitent sinner commits is heaped up against the day of wrath when he or she will experience the fullness of God's just judgment. Bad bad has no redeeming benefit for those who commit it.

Good Bad

It is this category with which we are most concerned when we seek to understand Paul's promise that "all things work together for good to those who love God" and "are the called according to His purpose." The bad that we experience is redeemed in the providence of God. This means that God brings good out of the evil we experience. Again, to say that all things work together for good is not the same thing as saying that all the things that happen to us are, when considered in themselves, good things. Yet if these things are working together for our good, then in an ultimate sense it is good that they happen to us. These bad things are truly bad things. But they are only *proximately* bad things; they are not *ultimately* bad things. They are blessings in disguise.

Often these "blessings" are exceedingly well disguised, so well disguised that we scant can see the slightest possible good in them. We have no more insight into the secret counsel of God than Joseph did when he endured the multitude of bad things that happened to him. What we do have is a divine promise that these bad things within the providence of God are being used by God for our good. The blessings may indeed be heavily veiled by disguise, but they are blessings nevertheless.

Blessing and Tragedy

To call tragedies blessings in disguise may smack of the worst sort of Pollyannaism as we glibly sing "Que Sera, Sera" with a maudlin happy face. It is easy to say, "It is the will of God" when tragedy strikes, but it is difficult to believe it firmly.

The tragedy may be real, but it is temporary and less than ultimate. For the Christian every tragedy is ultimately a blessing, or God is a liar. I once had a distressing experience as a seminary student. I was selected to deliver a sermon in chapel on a day when the entire presbytery was in attendance. I preached on the subject of original sin. At the conclusion of the sermon I was waylaid by three faculty members and the academic dean. They were livid. The dean was so angry at my sermon that he physically pushed me up against the wall in full view of the students and presbyters present. He berated me and humiliated me in that moment; my embarrassment was acute. When I finally escaped his clutches I rushed upstairs to the office of the faculty member whom I respected the most and told him of what had just transpired. A broad smile crossed his face, and in a kind tone he said to me, "How blessed you are to have undergone this experience."

I thought he must be joking, but I could feel he was speaking in earnest. I certainly didn't feel very blessed!

"How could I be blessed by this?" I asked him.

He answered, "Did not our Lord promise us, 'Blessed are those who are persecuted for righteousness' sake'?" He went on to applaud my sermon and said every saint from the apostle Paul to the great Princeton theologian B. B. Warfield, who were in heaven, rejoiced at the sermon I had preached.

Since I am mentioning an incident that took place over thirty years ago, it is obvious that I haven't forgotten it. The professor's remarks stuck in my memory bank, and I have recalled them on many similar occasions. Of course I should not have needed to have this professor remind me of the promise of Christ. The Lord's beatitude itself should have been sufficient.

In theory it is easy to understand the premise that all things work together for good to those who love God and are called according to His purpose, but to get this into our bloodstreams is another matter. It is one of the most difficult tasks of the practicing Christian. It involves not only believing in God but believing God.

In truth we may be confident that nothing bad will ever happen to us if we belong to Christ. This does not mean that nothing painful will ever happen. Our hearts may be broken a thousand times in this world, and our bodies wracked with pain. But these things are part of the Refiner's fire, the crucible of the kingdom of God.

When Augustine was advanced in years, he saw the storm clouds rising of the imminent invasion of the barbarians to the Roman Empire. He feared the marauding host would destroy the work he had labored to establish. He went to God in prayer and uttered a petition in three parts. He first asked that his people would be spared the devastation that could result from the barbarian invasion. Second, he asked that if that were not the will of God that he be given the grace to accept it. Finally, he prayed that in either case God would take him home soon. Augustine was obviously a man who believed Romans 8:28.

In contrast to the axiom that for the Christian every tragedy is ultimately a blessing is the predicament of the impenitent, or unrepenting, person. For that individual every blessing is a tragedy in disguise. God, in His common grace, pours abundant blessings upon unbelievers. His long-suffering sustains their very existence. But despite these many kindnesses, those who are impenitent continue in their rebellion against Him and maintain a steadfast posture of ingratitude. Indeed, this ingratitude stands at the very core of the indictment God makes against them, as we see in Romans:

> For the wrath of God is revealed from heaven against all ungodliness and unrighteousness of men, who suppress the truth in unrighteousness, because what may be known of God is manifest in them, for God has shown it to them. For since the creation of the world His invisible attributes are clearly seen, being understood by the things that are made, even His eternal power and Godhead, so that they are without excuse, because, although they knew God, they did not glorify Him as God, nor were thankful, but became futile in their thoughts, and their foolish hearts were darkened. (Rom. 1:18–21)

This text spells out the universal indictment: Natural man refuses to glorify God or to be thankful; this posture of ingratitude is sin and provokes the wrath of God. This wrath is augmented with every act of ingratitude toward the benevolence of God. In this regard the more grace and kindness the impenitent person receives from the hand of Providence, the more these blessings result in judgment. There is a limit to the long-suffering of God, as Paul declared to the Athenians:

"Truly, these times of ignorance God overlooked, but now commands all men everywhere to repent, because He has appointed a day on which He will judge the world in righteousness by the Man whom He has ordained. He has given assurance of this to all by raising Him from the dead." (Acts 17:30–31)

The appointed day of judgment marks the point in redemptive history when humanity's response to God's mercies is brought into account. On this day the blessings received by the impenitent will become tragedies, and the tragedies endured by the believer will be seen as blessings.

Enduring Evil for the Good of God

In his book *Charity and Its Fruits*, Jonathan Edwards considers the response Christians should have to slander and persecution against them. He focuses attention on the value of such personal suffering when measured against the value of the reward that flows from enduring such things. He reminds the reader of Jesus' teaching of the value of the individual soul compared with all the rewards this world has to offer. What will a man give in exchange for his soul? Jesus raised the question of ultimate profit, the "bottom line" of an earthly transaction, by asking, "What profit is it to a man if he gains the whole world, and loses his own soul?" (Matt. 16:26).

This question from the lips of Christ is rhetorical; its answer is clearly obvious: No profit ensues. Despite all the wealth in the world, the bottom line is written in red ink, and the "owner" is virtually bankrupt. His material blessings have become spiritual tragedies because he negotiated his soul in exchange for these goods. Such a Faustian bargain is no bargain at all because the merchandise received in the exchange is worthless compared with the value of the commodity traded for it.

In reverse fashion, Edwards reminds the reader that once our souls are secure in Christ and we have received the most valuable possession a person could possess, what possible tragedy could befall us at the hands of men to spoil the blessedness of our condition? The most we have to lose in this world by the assaults of the world, the flesh, and the devil is our physical and material well-being. We can lose our jobs, our health, our possessions, and even our reputations at the hands of our enemies. These things all seem tragic to us, and we labor to protect ourselves against such loss. But they cannot destroy our souls or the blessedness the Father has prepared for us from the foundation of the world. This was the idea that sustained Alexander Solzhenitsyn during his captivity, torture, and deprivation in the Russian Gulag. He knew his captors could take his life and in the process inflict pain and misery, but they could not touch his soul.

I once walked to the parking lot with one of my seminary professors after hearing an address that so distorted the teaching of John Calvin and so slandered the Reformer that I remarked, "If John Calvin had heard that he would have turned over in his grave." My professor stopped in midstride, turned to me, and said, "Don't you know that nothing could possibly disturb the felicity that John Calvin enjoys at this very moment?"

Many Christians have been called upon to endure great "evil" in this world. Though he was never martyred at the hands of his enemies, Martin Luther perhaps endured more calumnies and slander than any saint in history; he was one of the most hated men of his time. Anyone who is familiar with the biographical details of Luther's life is equally familiar with the torments of his soul. He

177

did not enjoy the loss of his peace and reputation; it grieved him deeply when some of his closest friends turned against him. Yet he found his solace in a mighty fortress. He sought his shelter in God. In the hymn he wrote around this theme drawn from Psalm 46, Luther wrote, "Let goods and kindred go, this mortal life also."

For Luther these were not empty words to be mouthed to the accompaniment of the full diapason of a church organ. For him they were integral to his creed. He was willing to lose all his goods for the sake of the gospel. He was willing to let go of "kindred," a term that refers both to family and to friends. He was fully prepared to abandon his own mortal life, but what he would not let go, what he would not give up, was the blessing of the gospel; he was prepared to incur the wrath of the whole world in its defense. What he did not want to lose, and was not willing to negotiate, was Christ.

This view toward enduring the evil of this world for the good of God was not unique to Luther, Calvin, and Edwards. It was characteristic of the saints of the Old Testament, as is recalled by the author of Hebrews:

> And what more shall I say? For the time would fail me to tell of Gideon and Barak and Samson and Jephthah, also of David and Samuel and the prophets: who through faith subdued kingdoms, worked righteousness, obtained promises, stopped the mouths of lions, quenched the violence of fire, escaped the edge of the sword, out of weakness were made strong, became valiant in battle, turned to flight the armies of the aliens. Women received their dead raised to life again.
>
> Others were tortured, not accepting deliverance, that they might obtain a better resurrection. Still others had trial of mockings and scourgings, yes, and of chains and imprisonment. They were stoned, they were sawn in two, were tempted, were slain with the sword. They wandered about in sheepskins and goatskins, being destitute, afflicted, tormented—of whom the world was not worthy. They wandered in deserts and mountains, in dens and caves of the earth. (Heb. 11:32–38)

The assessment of Scripture regarding these people who, as children of Providence, endured "good evil" for His sake is that the world was not worthy of them.

Chapter 18

Providence and Miracles

CHRISTIANITY IS A FAITH THAT IS BASED UPON AND ROOTED in miracles. Take away miracles, and you take away Christianity. Church history is replete with attempts to do this. From the attempts of the Enlightenment thinkers to reduce Christianity to a form of naturalism, to the biblical vandalism of nineteenth-century Liberalism to explain away biblical miracles with fancifully contrived ethical parables, to Bultmann's systematic program of "de-mythologizing," the attacks have been relentless.

Excising the biblical accounts of miracles is an exercise in revisionism, a kind of canon reductionism. Like the ancient heretic Marcion, who produced an abridged version of the New Testament canon in which all references to the Old Testament God were deleted in order to satisfy Marcion's own aversion to that deity, so modern scholars, embarrassed and scandalized by biblical miracles, have sought to reconstruct a religion without them. Whatever kind of religion results is not the Christian religion. Christianity stands or falls with the biblical account of miracles. Without miracles there is no Exodus. Without miracles there is no resurrection. With no resurrection our faith is in vain.

As early as the first century, Paul had to do battle with skeptics of the miraculous and the supernatural. First Corinthians 15 is a case in point. Here Paul responds to those who want a Christianity without miraculous resurrection. He pushes the logic of such a position by using the ancient method of logical argument called *reductio ad absurdum* reasoning:

> Moreover, brethren, I declare to you the gospel which I preached to you, which also you received and in which you stand, by which also you are saved, if you hold fast that word which I preached to you—unless you believed in vain.
>
> For I delivered to you first of all that which I also received: that Christ died for our sins according to the Scriptures, and that He was buried, and that He rose again the third day according to the Scriptures, and that He was seen by Cephas, then by the twelve. After that He was seen by over five hundred brethren at once, of whom the greater part remain to the present, but some have fallen asleep. After that He was seen by James, then by all the apostles. Then last of all He was seen by me also, as by one born out of due time.
>
> For I am the least of the apostles, who am not worthy to be called an apostle, because I persecuted the church of God. But by the grace of God I am what I am, and His grace toward me was not in vain; but I labored more abundantly than they all, yet not I, but the grace of God which was with me. Therefore, whether it was I or they, so we preach and so you believed.
>
> Now if Christ is preached that He has been raised from the dead, how do some among you say that there is no resurrection of the dead? But if there is no resurrection of the dead, then Christ is not risen. And if Christ is not risen, then our preaching is empty and your faith is also empty. Yes, and we are found false witnesses of God, because we have testified of God that He raised up Christ, whom He did not raise up—if in fact the dead do not rise. For if the dead do not rise, then Christ is not risen. And if Christ is not risen, your faith is futile; you are still in your sins! (1 Cor. 15:1–17)

In this extended argument Paul first affirms the gospel and

exhorts his readers to hold fast to it. He speaks of a "tradition" that had been handed over by the apostles. This is the apostolic tradition, which is the very foundation of the church. The specific tradition Paul has in view is the account of the resurrection of Christ, which fulfilled the Old Testament Scriptures and was verified by the eyewitness testimony of the apostles. After providing a summary of this eyewitness testimony, Paul adds himself to the list of eyewitnesses of the risen Christ. Then he proceeds to argue the consequences of a resurrection-less or miracle-less Christianity. The penultimate conclusion of this argument is found in verse 17, where Paul gave the if-then argument: "If Christ is not risen, your faith is futile."

Paul stresses the futility of constructing a Christian faith without miracles because the resurrection of Christ certainly fits into the "miracle" category. But, what exactly is the miracle category? What do we mean when we speak of miracles? Much confusion persists about this concept. There are those who argue that miracles occurred in biblical times but do not occur today. There are those who argue that miracles did not occur in biblical times and in fact never occur. There are those who argue that miracles occurred in biblical times and still are occurring today.

Part of the problem we face with these disparate views is that there is disagreement regarding the nature of miracles. Naturalists reject miracles because naturalists, by definition, reject the supernatural and regard miracles as intrusions from the supernatural realm, which they deny exists at all. Naturalists operate with a world view that has no room or allowance for even the possibility of miracles. This position collides head-on with biblical Christianity and involves a dispute between two utterly irreconcilable world views.

However, even within the context of the Christian world view there is still the debate about whether miracles such as those recorded in sacred Scripture still occur today. The question is clouded by variant definitions of *miracle*. Most of those involved in this debate agree on several points, including: (1) God, in His providential government of the universe, is able to perform miracles. There is no dispute about the possibility of God to work in a manner that differs from His ordinary providence. (2) God did, in fact, perform miracles in the past, as recorded in the Bible. (3) Miracles are supernatural works of God, and (4) God is still working supernaturally today. All of these points are agreed upon by those who disagree on the question of whether God is still working miracles.

Here the definition of miracle becomes crucial. Some people loosely call all the works that have their ultimate causal power in God "miracles." For example, we often hear it said that the birth of a baby is a miracle. Now, surely the birth of a baby is an awe-inspiring thing. It snaps our attention to the amazing reality of life itself. But there is nothing unusual or extraordinary about the birth of a baby. Literally millions of such incidences occur every day all around the world.

I find it almost impossible not to be transfixed when I see a deer in the wild. I have had this experience hundreds, if not thousands, of times. But I never find it boring because I am taken by the beauty and grace of these creatures. The same may be said about the magnificence of sunsets, which provoke thoughts within me of the glorious majesty of God, who displays Himself in the beauty of His creation.

But in biblical terms a deer in the woods is not a miracle; nor is a sunset a miracle. They are normal parts of the natural realm that point beyond the natural realm to the supernatural God who makes them. Likewise, the birth of a baby is not usually considered within the theological category of miracle.

We usually can agree that all miracles are *supernatural events.* But the question remains, are all supernatural events miracles? Some people reverse these propositions and see them as tautological; that is, some would define a miracle as any supernatural event wrought by God. Luther, for example, routinely described as a miracle the divine work of regeneration, the supernatural work of the Holy Spirit that is wrought immediately in the soul of a human being. By "immediately" I don't mean "suddenly" (though it is that too) but rather a work that God the Holy Spirit works without the aid of some natural medium. He does not depend upon secondary causes for this effect but effects this spiritual transformation of the soul by the sole and immediate power of His own.

Part of the problem with reaching agreement on the definition of a miracle is that the Bible does not have a single word that explicitly is restricted to the English word *miracle*. Surely some English translations of the Bible contain the word *miracle* but that is a matter of the translator's choice of nomenclature. The *concept* of miracle is derived from three distinct biblical terms, which may be translated "signs," "powers," and "wonders." The theological concept of miracle is then extrapolated from the use of these terms in the Bible.

Technically, *signs, wonders,* and *powers* are not synonyms, and we fall into certain dangers when we seek to use them interchangeably, though they are often quite closely related. The marvelous works of God recorded in Scripture certainly manifest His power. They also evoke wonder from those who behold them. One of the most common words that attends the accounts of the miracles of Christ is the word *astonished*, or *amazed*. The word *sign* is used frequently for the works of Jesus, especially in the Gospel of John.

A sign is something that points beyond itself to something else. When we approach the city of Orlando, we may read a road sign that declares "Orlando." This sign announces the border, or edge, of the city; it is included within the city but it is not the city. For an event to be regarded as a sign it must have "significance"; it must point to something beyond itself.

When we consider the *purpose* of biblical miracles, we see that there are many. God used miracles to deliver the Israelites from their bondage in Egypt. Jesus used His miracles to alleviate suffering and to give sight to the blind, hearing to the deaf, etc. But these immediate purposes did not exhaust the purpose of these works. They also served as signs. They pointed to something else beyond the function at hand. One of the most important, if not the most important, function of biblical miracles was to attest to agents of revelation. They provided what John Locke called the "credit of the proposer."

One example of this is shown in the New Testament account of Nicodemus coming to Jesus:

> There was a man of the Pharisees named Nicodemus, a ruler of the Jews. This man came to Jesus by night and said to Him, "Rabbi, we know that You are a teacher come from God; for no one can do these signs that You do unless God is with him." (John 3:1–2)

Because we have an inspired record of what Nicodemus said does not mean we can infer that his judgment regarding Jesus was an inspired judgment or that the inference he declared is valid. Though Nicodemus was expressing his fallible human judgment about the matter, he was expressing a conclusion that is consistent with the Bible itself. He concluded that Jesus was a teacher sent from God because Jesus performed miracles. That was the only conclusion he could come to if his premise was correct that "no one can do these signs unless God is with him." This raises the whole question of whether people or devils who are not sent by God can also perform miracles. We will take that up in the next chapter. For now we simply observe that Nicodemus uttered a universal negative proposition with an exceptive clause added to it. His universal negative proposition was that no one could (or was able) to perform these works without some necessary condition first being met. The necessary condition is indicated by the word *unless.* The necessary condition was the help of God.

If Nicodemus was correct, then we understand that one of the most significant points of the biblical miracle is its attesting to agents who are sent from and speak for God. This important function of the biblical concept of miracles is not demonstrated solely by the judgment and testimony of Nicodemus. In Hebrews we read:

> Therefore we must give the more earnest heed to the things we have heard, lest we drift away. For if the word spoken through

angels proved steadfast, and every transgression and disobedience received a just reward, how shall we escape if we neglect so great a salvation, which at the first began to be spoken by the Lord, and was confirmed to us by those who heard Him, God also bearing witness both with signs and wonders, with various miracles, and gifts of the Holy Spirit, according to His own will? (Heb. 2:1–4)

Here God bears witness to the apostolic testimony by confirming it with signs and wonders. This idea is deeply rooted in the Old Testament, as may be seen with the problem Moses encountered when he met God in the Midianite desert:

> Then Moses answered and said, "But suppose they will not believe me or listen to my voice; suppose they say, 'The LORD has not appeared to you.'"
> So the LORD said to him, "What is that in your hand?"
> He said, "A rod."
> And He said, "Cast it on the ground." So he cast it on the ground, and it became a serpent; and Moses fled from it. Then the LORD said to Moses, "Reach out your hand and take it by the tail" (and he reached out his hand and caught it, and it became a rod in his hand), "that they may believe that the LORD God of their fathers, the God of Abraham, the God of Isaac, and the God of Jacob, has appeared to you." (Exod. 4:1–5)

Moses was faced with a problem of credibility on two fronts. The first problem he had was to convince Pharaoh to set free the entire slave-labor force that was so important to his national economy. Pharaoh was hardly likely to do that on the sage advice of an aged shepherd from the wilderness! The second problem Moses had was to persuade a powerless horde of humanity to follow him in the biggest wildcat strike in recorded history. This was a credibility problem with a vengeance! When Moses asked God how it would be possible for him to overcome this credibility problem God's answer was to equip Moses with the power to perform miracles, which did ultimately persuade the people of Israel—and Pharaoh—that Moses was sent from God.

As we seek a precise definition for *miracle*, we must not only include its function as a sign or as attestation of spokesmen for God (agents of revelation), but we must also observe that biblical miracles were actions and events that were observable in the external world. As Paul declared to Herod Agrippa, "This thing was not done in a corner" (Acts 26:26). The biblical miracles were public and open to scrutiny, unlike the miraculous "attestation" of self-proclaimed prophets like the Mormon Joseph Smith. Christianity is not a mystery religion whose revelation is restricted to an elite secret group of initiates.

To avoid such confusion and to protect against a retreat into claims that cannot be verified or falsified by public witnesses, the biblical miracles were staged in the external world. Reformed theology historically defined miracles as those supernatural acts performed in the external, perceivable world by the immediate power of God, producing supernatural and extraordinary effects that only God can do. In Romans Paul speaks of God's ability to bring something out of nothing and life out of death, a power that no creature possesses.

Sometimes the definition of miracle is expressed in shorthand terms as a work that is against the normal laws of nature, an action that is *contra naturam*. This is a useful distinction as long as we are careful to remember that nature's laws are God's laws and that they do not operate independently from Him. Nature, even in the ordinary daily operations we perceive, is always subject to Supernature. If the laws of nature are the providential will of God, they can hardly be "violated," because God does not violate Himself.

By this we see that the *contra* used in the Latin term actually refers to the difference between God's ordinary providence and His extraordinary providence. Though He normally works in one way, which we call *ordinary* because it is usual and customary, He is still able to work in unusual or *extraordinary* ways as well.

As human beings we are daily working against the "laws" of

nature. When we lift heavy weights from the ground we do not suspend or violate the law of gravity. Rather, we simply counteract it by a stronger force; the forces we use are finite and unlimited. We are potent but not omnipotent. These same laws can be counteracted by an omnipotent force that exceeds anything we can ordinarily accomplish ourselves. We lack the power to make ax heads float or turn water into wine. We are able to swim in the water but not walk upon the water. Such activities are indeed extraordinary and carry the sign of the miraculous.

Miracles by God's Commands

That miracles are wrought by the immediate power of God may be debated in light of some of the miracles found in the Bible. For example, in the miracle of the crossing of the Red Sea a natural force was used as a medium for the event. The Bible describes it:

> Then Moses stretched out his hand over the sea; and the LORD caused the sea to go back by a strong east wind all that night, and made the sea into dry land, and the waters were divided. So the children of Israel went into the midst of the sea on the dry ground, and the waters were a wall to them on their right hand and on their left. And the Egyptians pursued and went after them into the midst of the sea, all Pharaoh's horses, his chariots, and his horsemen.
>
> Now it came to pass, in the morning watch, that the LORD looked down upon the army of the Egyptians through the pillar of fire and cloud, and He troubled the army of the Egyptians. And He took off their chariot wheels, so that they drove them with difficulty; and the Egyptians said, "Let us flee from the face of Israel, for the LORD fights for them against the Egyptians."
>
> Then the LORD said to Moses, "Stretch out your hand over the sea, that the waters may come back upon the Egyptians, on their chariots, and on their horsemen." And Moses stretched out his hand over the sea; and when the morning appeared, the sea returned to its full depth, while the Egyptians were fleeing into it.

So the LORD overthrew the Egyptians in the midst of the sea. (Exod. 14:21–27)

In this episode, at Moses' signal God caused a powerful wind to blow, so powerful that it opened a path in the sea by creating a passageway bounded by a wall of water on both sides. God used a secondary cause, the medium of the wind, to effect the miracle, but the immediate cause was His divine command. It is one thing for such a wind to blow; it is another for it to blow in such a manner on command.

This type of miracle-by-command is seen also in the New Testament account of Jesus' calming the sea and stilling the storm. It is not extraordinary for winds to stop blowing and seas to stop raging; that happens with regularity. Indeed, the sea's becoming suddenly calm is not so rare that this event in itself would be particularly noteworthy. The sea's becoming calm at the command of a human being would be extraordinary. We must admit, however, that such an event could take place by what we call sheer coincidence. We could fall into the informal fallacy of *post hoc ergo propter hoc*, after this, therefore because of this. The rooster may crow just before dawn, but simply because the appearance of the dawn follows in close proximity to the crowing of the rooster does not mean that the rooster causes the sun to rise.

If Jesus' only recorded miracle was the calming of the storm on command, we would legitimately be tempted to assume that the conjunction of events was sheer coincidence. But in the blaze of miracles that followed in the wake of Christ, we would be foolish to assume it was a coincidence. That was not the conclusion of the disciples who witnessed it; even these men who had witnessed other miracles by Jesus were astonished by this one. It followed the pattern of power on command reminiscent of God's calling the world into existence and of Jesus' calling Lazarus from the dead.

The debate among Christians over whether God performs miracles today centers on the narrow definition of *miracle*. We will consider that question, along with the question of satanic miracles, in the next chapter.

Chapter 19

Counterfeit Miracles

THE ISSUE SURROUNDING THE QUESTION OF WHETHER GOD performs miracles today is complex and often inflammatory. If a person in the evangelical camp declares that he does not believe in contemporary miracles he is often looked upon with suspicion. The suspicion arises because unbelief in miracles is associated with naturalism, skepticism, or Liberalism. (I use the capital L for Liberal to refer to a distinct school of theology and not to a person who in some other way may be regarded as liberal.)

Since a cardinal point of dispute between Liberalism and evangelicalism involves biblical miracles, the dispute spills over into the question of modern miracles as well. There is a tendency here to assign guilt by association; because Liberalism does not believe that miracles occur today we tend to think that anyone who denies that miracles occur today must be a Liberal. The key difference between evangelicals and Liberals on the question of miracles is not whether they occur today but whether they occurred in the past, as the Bible contends.

John Calvin, for example, is rarely considered a Liberal. Calvin and Luther, at the time of the Reformation, were repeatedly challenged by the Roman Catholic Church to produce miracles that would authenticate their teaching. Rome appealed to its documented miracles of the saints as proof that God was speaking through the Roman Catholic Church and not through the Reformers. For their part, the Reformers denied that the apostolic office continued in the church or that the church was the source of new divine revelation.

The debate over continuing revelation was critical to the Reformation position of *Sola Scriptura*, the belief that Scriptures were sufficient and the only source of written special revelation. Rome argued that a second source of such special revelation occurred in the tradition of the church; this dual source of revelation was decreed at the Council of Trent in the sixteenth century and reaffirmed by the papal encyclical of Pius XII, *Humani Generis*, in the twentieth century. Rome, aware of the biblical significance of miracles' proving or attesting to agents of revelation, could appeal to the church's miracles to support its claim that it was the true church and that the Reformers were false prophets.

This question of the Reformers' lack of miracles was mentioned by Calvin in his letter to the king of France that introduces his famous *Institutes of the Christian Religion*. Calvin says:

> In demanding miracles from us, they act dishonestly; for we have not coined some new gospel, but retain the very one the truth of which is confirmed by all the miracles which Christ and the apostles ever wrought. But they have a peculiarity which we have not—they can confirm their faith by constant miracles down to the present day! Nay rather, they allege miracles which might produce wavering in minds otherwise well disposed; they are so frivolous and ridiculous, so vain and false. (p. 8)

The magisterial Reformers argued that their doctrine was confirmed by the authority of the Bible. We notice in these arguments that neither Rome nor the Reformers challenged the premise that miracles function as signs that authenticate agents of revelation; they agreed on that point. The point in dispute was whether revelation continued beyond the apostolic age and with the continuing revelation the continuing attestation via miracle. Calvin and Luther challenged the authenticity, not only of Rome's teaching and her claim to continuing apostolic authority and revelation, but the authenticity of their claimed miracles. The Reformers considered the miracles of Rome to be not only frivolous but counterfeit. They denied that they were real miracles at all.

One thing is clear about this dispute. The issue was not whether God could perform miracles but whether the Bible was the sole source of inscripturated special revelation. That point is often overlooked in the current debate about continuing miracles. Within evangelicalism today, especially but not exclusively in the charismatic wing, claims are being made of new revelation from God and the abundant presence of new miracles. The possibility of modern miracles is considered so great that posters are sold in Christian bookstores and adorn the studies of many pastors that read "Expect a Miracle!" In these circles miracles are not only considered possible, they are expected. Evangelists promise miracles at their revival services and even claim to perform them on national television.

We must also be careful to note that many evangelicals are persuaded that revelation does not continue to this day but miracles do. They divorce miracles from revelation on the assumption that we can have miracle workers without revelation as others argue that you can have revelation without miracles. Since miracles have other functions beside as attesting agents of revelation they can continue without any corresponding revelation.

The classic Reformed position on this matter agrees that miracles have other functions besides attesting to agents of revelation, as we have seen. That is, miracles can do more than attest to agents of revelation. But the question remains, Can they do less? Herein lies the problem. If a non-agent of revelation is able to perform miracles, how can miracles ever function as proof of attestation of an agent of revelation? If both agents of revelation and non-agents of revelation can perform miracles, what possible attesting value can there ever be in a miracle? If a false prophet can perform a miracle, the true prophet cannot appeal to miracles as proof of his own office. The problem becomes all the more acute when we see that the New Testament does appeal to the miracles of the apostles as proof of their authority, which is clearly a spurious appeal and false argument if it is true that non-agents of revelation can do miracles.

I was once invited to speak at a meeting of Christian booksellers at the time when Benny Hinn's book *Good Morning, Holy Spirit* was the number one bestseller in the Christian marketplace. I asked, if Hinn was doing the miracles he claimed he was doing, why was no one advocating that his book be added to the New Testament canon? Hinn claimed new revelation, that God even spoke audibly to him; thus he had all the claimed credentials of a biblical prophet.

One of the things that is conspicuously absent in the repertoire of modern miracle workers is the type of miracles that were per-formed by biblical agents of revelation. Benny Hinn performs his miracles on a stage with theatrical accouterments that would have scandalized the apostles. He does not perform his miracles in the cemetery. What miracle worker today is able to turn water into wine or raise people from the dead who have been dead for four days? Benny Hinn cannot part the Red Sea or cause ax heads to float. Why not? Is the quality of miracle that survives to this day less than those performed by biblical agents of revelation? Has the arm of the Lord waxed short?

It is clear that however we define a miracle we must place the alleged miracles of today in a different class, or category, from those recorded in the Scriptures. No one is bringing something out of nothing these days—unless it is the currency produced by the fed-eral government!

Does this mean then that God in His providence no longer is working? Has God ceased and desisted from exerting His supernat-ural power in our midst? Does God not answer prayers in extraordinary ways or grant requests for healing when doctors say such healing cannot occur? By no means! God is still alive and working. He answers the prayers of His people in remarkable ways.

His supernatural grace is evident among us every day. If we consider these things miracles then we must admit that miracles are still going on.

We distinguish three categories of issues raised by the function of miracles to attest to agents of revelation and authenticate His written Word. These categories include His normal providence, His extraordinary providence, and His miracles (in the narrow sense defined already). Within these three categories we say that God continues His work of ordinary providence and His work of extraordinary providence but not His work of attesting to agents of special revelation with miracles in the narrow sense.

Satanic Miracles

The question remains: What about the miracles of Satan? Does not the Bible teach that Satan, the Great Deceiver, can also perform miracles? Let us look at some of the relevant texts of Scripture that raise this question:

> If there arises among you a prophet or a dreamer of dreams, and he gives you a sign or a wonder, and the sign or the wonder comes to pass, of which he spoke to you, saying, "Let us go after other gods"—which you have not known—"and let us serve them," you shall not listen to the words of that prophet or that dreamer of dreams, for the LORD your God is testing you to know whether you love the LORD your God with all your heart and with all your soul. (Deut. 13:1–3)

> Many will say to Me in that day, "Lord, Lord, have we not prophesied in Your name, cast out demons in Your name, and done many wonders in Your name?" And then I will declare to them, "I never knew you; depart from Me, you who practice lawlessness!" (Matt. 7:22–23)

> Then if anyone says to you, "Look, here is the Christ!" or "There!" do not believe it. For false christs and false prophets will

rise and show great signs and wonders to deceive, if possible, even the elect. See, I have told you beforehand.

Therefore if they say to you, "Look, He is in the desert!" do not go out; or "Look, He is in the inner rooms!" do not believe it." (Matt. 24:23–26)

The coming of the lawless one is according to the working of Satan, with all power, signs, and lying wonders, and with all unrighteous deception among those who perish, because they did not receive the love of the truth, that they might be saved. And for this reason God will send them strong delusion, that they should believe the lie, that they all may be condemned who did not believe the truth but had pleasure in unrighteousness. (2 Thess. 2:9–12)

This sampling of biblical texts calls attention to the sober warning of the powers and deception of Satan. His first appearance as the serpent in Eden was marked by guile and craftiness, and he continues to be a formidable adversary for the people of God. As Luther said, "His power and craft are great," and since it is coupled with "cruel hate" it becomes all the more dangerous. Satan is so masterful in the art of deception that he is capable of appearing to us *sub species boni*, or under the auspices of the good. He can transform himself into an angel of light, and he seeks to deceive even "the elect" (see Matt. 24:24 and Mark 13:22).

The Scriptures portray Satan as a higher being than we are. He is an angelic being, albeit a fallen angel. As such, strictly speaking, he is not a supernatural being. He may be higher than what we expect to see in ordinary "nature," but he still belongs to the natural order in the sense that he is a creature and part of the creaturely order of nature. He is not on the level with God and possesses no incommunicable divine attributes. He is a spirit being but a finite spirit. He is not infinite, eternal, immutable, omniscient, or omnipresent. He may have more knowledge than we have and greater power, but he does not have divine power.

When the Bible speaks of Satan's alleged "miracles," his works are called "signs and lying wonders" (2 Thess. 2:9). The question is this, What is meant by the qualifying term *lying*? Does this mean that Satan can perform actual miracles in a lying cause? Or does it mean that the signs and wonders he performs are lying in that they are fraudulent tricks and not actual miracles? Theologians are divided on this question.

Some who believe that Satan can perform actual miracles in the sense that he can do works that are *contra naturam* argue that these works are not *contra peccatum,* or "against sin." This technical distinction is designed to show that although Satan can act against nature he can never, or at least won't ever, act against his own evil purposes, which are "pro-sin" rather than "contra-sin." The reasoning is that a house divided against itself will not stand, and Satan will never work against his own aims by doing miracles. His miracles are always directed against the good and the truth of Christ. We are told by advocates of this view that we can discern the difference between the miracles of Satan and the miracles of God by subjecting them to the test of Scripture.

This argument suffers from a fatal fallacy, the fallacy of circular reasoning, or question-begging. Before we can ever test the miracles of Satan by the content of Scripture, we must first have a Scripture by which to test them. We remember that Scripture is attested to by the miracles performed by agents of revelation that certify they are spokesmen from God. But how do we know that the miracles that attested them were not satanic? Perhaps Nicodemus should have amended his statement to read, "We know that you are a teacher sent from God or the devil or you would not be able to do the works that you do." Indeed, the Pharisees made that very charge against Jesus, that He was performing His miracles by the power of Satan. At this point their theology was inferior to that of Nicodemus, who was more restrictive in his view of *miracle.*

The same problem we encountered with the question of miracles performed by non-agents of revelation is exaggerated by the problem of satanic miracles. If Satan can perform real miracles, then the biblical appeal to miracles as certification that the miracle workers come from God is a spurious appeal.

I think it makes more sense to conclude that the "lying" that describes Satan's signs and wonders describes not only their aim but their character. They are lying signs in that they are fraudulent and fake. His signs resemble the astounding tricks performed by the magicians of Egypt who sought to duplicate the powers of Moses:

> Then the LORD spoke to Moses and Aaron, saying, "When Pharaoh speaks to you, saying, 'Show a miracle for yourselves,' then you shall say to Aaron, 'Take your rod and cast it before Pharaoh, and let it become a serpent.'" So Moses and Aaron went in to Pharaoh, and they did so, just as the LORD commanded. And Aaron cast down his rod before Pharaoh and before his servants, and it became a serpent.
>
> But Pharaoh also called the wise men and the sorcerers; so the magicians of Egypt, they also did in like manner with their enchantments. For every man threw down his rod, and they became serpents. But Aaron's rod swallowed up their rods. (Exod. 7:8–12)

The magicians of Egypt had no more magic than magicians have today. The difference is that most modern magicians in the Western world do not really claim to perform magic but are quite willing to call themselves "illusionists," or masters of sleight of hand. Magic stores abound where those interested in this modern form of entertainment can learn many tricks of the trade. I once had a neighbor who was a cabinetmaker. His specialty was in making special cabinets for performing magicians. They contained clever hinge mechanisms, false bottoms, secret panels, and often mirrors. Magicians today have no trouble concealing a rabbit in a hat or even a snake in a collapsible tube. When Moses and Aaron performed their miracles, the magicians of Egypt thought they could duplicate their feats. But not only were their serpents swallowed up in the process, they were chagrined when they soon ran out of their bag of tricks and could not duplicate the feats of genuine miracle workers.

Some of the tricks performed by modern magicians are truly amazing to those who witness them. The irony is that though many of them require great skill and years of careful practice some of the most amazing feats they perform are at the same time some of the simplest to execute.

Lou Costello would win a lot of money in bets when he would produce a normal deck of cards and ask his "pigeon" to select any card from the deck. Then he told his friend he knew a man in a distant city who was a bona fide mind reader. He would bet that if the man called the mind reader on the phone and asked for the wizard that the wizard could tell him which card he had selected by long-distance mental telepathy. When the sucker took the bet (as Jackie Gleason once admitted he did) he would call the number and ask for the wizard. The wizard would tell the man to think of the card he had selected and then promptly tell him the card over the phone . . . It worked every time.

How did Costello or the wizard do it? It was a simple scam. Costello had fifty-two designated "wizards" around the country. Each one was responsible for one particular card. Costello memorized the wizard and his phone number for all fifty-two cards in the deck. When his pigeon selected a card, Costello simply gave him the name of the wizard responsible for that card. Anytime that person received a phone call from someone asking for the wizard, he knew what card he was supposed to identify.

Satan's tricks are far more sophisticated than that, but they remain tricks nevertheless. His prestidigitation may exceed that of Houdini but it nowhere approaches the miraculous power of God, who alone can bring something out of nothing and life out of death.

Satan's minions lost their contest with Moses and Aaron. They were defeated by Elijah at Mount Carmel. And they were no match for Christ in the wilderness or during His earthly ministry. Satan sought to entice Jesus to use His genuine miraculous power in the service of Satan, a power Satan coveted. Simon Magus sought to purchase the power of the Holy Spirit to no avail (see Acts 8:9).

The providence of God is served by the power of God. Miracles are a part of His sovereign rule over the creation and over history. His Word is sovereignly attested to by that power that He is unwilling to grant to the powers of darkness. The tricks of Satan are exposed by the Word, whose truth has been confirmed and verified by the miraculous attestation of God.

The church today faces a grave threat from those who want to claim apostolic power and apostolic authority. In this regard the Christian must be ever vigilant and flee from those who make such claims.

Chapter 20

Providence and Prayer

IF GOD IN HIS PROVIDENCE ORDAINS ALL THAT COMES TO pass, why should the Christian pray? On the surface the doctrine of providence may suggest that prayer is an exercise in futility. Beside the clear and obvious reality that we are frequently commanded to pray there stands many reasons for us to be ardently involved in the exercise of prayer.

We remember that God has an eternal plan of redemption, a plan that is formed down to the smallest details. God has a purpose, end, and goal to that plan of redemption. All things are not only working together for our good, but they are also working together for the accomplishment of God's eternal purpose. His providence not only extends to the ends but also to the means to those ends. A means is a vehicle through which something is accomplished. So, simply stated, God ordains the means to the ends as well as the ends themselves. He uses the means as secondary causes under the supervision and government of His primary causality.

In the life of the church we speak of the "means of grace." One of the chief means of grace is prayer. The means of grace are given to us as instruments for our sanctification. Prayer is a vital vehicle, or tool, that God has given His church so that we may become fully sanctified. By prayer our thoughts are lifted toward Him and our hearts are bent to His perfect will. God is not the beneficiary of our prayers. He is the Benefactor; we are the beneficiaries.

Calvin remarked in the *Institutes*:

> But some will say, Does he not know without a monitor for both what our difficulties are, and what is meet for our interest, so that it seems in some measure superfluous to solicit him by our prayers, as if he were winking, or even sleeping, until aroused by the sound of our voice? Those who argue thus attend not to the end for which the Lord taught us to pray. It was not so much for his sake as for ours. (III/XX.3)

What possible benefit could our prayers have for God? He has no need of them for self-fulfillment. The praise and adoration of His creatures, though He declares it pleasing to Him, are not things He requires for His own divine fulfillment. He is altogether self-sufficient, and His own felicity can be neither augmented nor diminished by the works of His creatures. He is the ever-blessed God who got along without us before we were created and can get along without us now.

Can our prayers add to God's knowledge? To ask this question is to answer it. God is omniscient. He gleans no new information from us that He did not already have. We are not His research assistants who gather information for Him because He lacks it. He knows what we need before we tell Him and knows even what it is we are about to tell Him before we speak a word in prayer. As the psalmist wrote:

> O LORD, You have searched me and known me.
> You know my sitting down and my rising up;
> You understand my thought afar off.
> You comprehend my path and my lying down,
> And are acquainted with all my ways.
> For there is not a word on my tongue,
> But behold, O LORD, You know it altogether. (Ps. 139:1–4)

Nor do we function as God's guidance counselors; we are never in a position to correct God's judgments. As we have already seen, God has no need of a Plan B, a fall-back course to put into operation when the initial plan fails or is thwarted.

Prayer does not change God's mind . . . ever. Why not? Precisely because He can learn nothing new from us and because He never has a plan that is less than perfect. I change my mind on planned courses of action when I receive new information or when I discover an error in my thinking. These situations are simply not possible for God.

Though prayer never changes God's mind in the ultimate sense, it does not follow that prayer is a useless exercise that accomplishes nothing. On the contrary, the New Testament makes it clear that prayer is a powerful force and that it is a force for change:

> Confess your trespasses to one another, and pray for one another, that you may be healed. The effective, fervent prayer of a righteous man avails much. Elijah was a man with a nature like ours, and he prayed earnestly that it would not rain; and it did not rain on the land for three years and six months. And he prayed again, and the heaven gave rain, and the earth produced its fruit. (James 5:16–18)

In this text James declares that the "effective, fervent prayer of a righteous man avails much." The apostle uses qualifiers here that are important. He speaks of prayer that is *effective* and prayer that is *fervent.* The two are related. Effective prayer is prayer that "works"; James says it "avails much." This promise does not apply to prayer that is cavalier or full of empty phrases or recited dispassionately. Saying that prayer is to be fervent is not a call to wild and frenzied emotionalism, which may be as empty as the vacuous prayers of those who express rote phrases. Fervency calls attention to a sincere and steadfast focus upon God; this kind of prayer is serious. It comes from the core of the soul, from the heart of the saint who means business.

James also says that effective prayer is the prayer of the righteous. Such prayers are a sweet-smelling savor to God, and the Lord is pleased to hear them. But the prayers of the ungodly are not so. Their prayers are uttered in hypocrisy and are a stench in the nostrils of God. Repeatedly God warns that He will not hear the prayers of the proud or the impenitent. It is not our sin that is the barrier to effective prayer; it is the attitude we have toward our sin that matters. God hears the prayers of sinners because, apart from the prayers of His Son, that is the only kind of people who pray. Here the righteous refer to those sinners covered by the righteousness of Christ who approach God. They are the justified who remain *simul justus et peccator*, at the same time just and sinner. If God listened only to the prayers of those who are completely righteous in themselves He would not listen to our pleadings.

James points to Elijah as an example of one "with a nature like ours." What does this mean? We may think it difficult to liken ourselves to such a titan of faith as the prophet Elijah. After all, there are so few ways in which we are like him. But we are like him at least to this degree: Elijah was a human being. He had no divine nature. He was also a fallen human being. In a word, Elijah was a justified sinner as we are ourselves if we are in Christ.

The point is simple: God not only listens to the petitions of the prophets, but He listens to ours as well. Otherwise, there would be no point in calling us to pray while at the same time pointing to Elijah as an example.

On numerous occasions Jesus called His disciples to pray and encouraged them to be bold and diligent in that exercise. The parable of the unjust judge is a case in point:

> Then He spoke a parable to them, that men always ought to pray and not lose heart, saying: "There was in a certain city a judge who did not fear God nor regard man. Now there was a widow in that city; and she came to him, saying, 'Get justice for me from my adversary.' And he would not for a while; but afterward he said within himself, 'Though I do not fear God nor regard man, yet because this widow troubles me I will avenge her, lest by her continual coming she weary me.'"

Then the Lord said, "Hear what the unjust judge said. And shall God not avenge His own elect who cry out day and night to Him, though He bears long with them?" (Luke 18:1–7)

Luke tells us the reason why Jesus spoke this parable. It was not to convince us that God can be persuaded to change His mind, as the unjust judge's mind was changed by the annoying pleas of the widow. It is a parable of contrast more than of comparison. Jesus gave the parable to teach that we ought always to pray and not lose heart. The point is that if an unjust judge will listen to the persistent pleas of a woman then *how much more* will the Just Judge of heaven and earth listen to our petitions?

Jesus promises that God will certainly vindicate or avenge His elect who cry out to Him day and night. This is part of the promise of God because it is part of the plan of God. As we pray we are not pestering God to hear us, but we are engaged in an exercise designed to benefit our own souls. We pray so that we may not lose heart.

When we understand James's words that prayer "avails much," we can conclude that prayer really does change things. Again, what it changes is not the eternal plan of God or the perfection of His knowledge. Most importantly, prayer changes *us*. Why else would Jesus instruct us to pray for those things that God already knows we need? Again, it is surely not for His instruction.

We may be tempted to say that what we receive from the hand of Providence is ultimately dependent upon certain conditions we must meet to receive it. Jesus warned that we have not because we ask not. This would seem to suggest that God's blessings are contingent, ultimately dependent upon us. But it is the character of God to meet for us the very conditions He demands from us. Faith is a condition for our justification. But it is a condition we meet only after God works faith in our hearts. He ensures, not only the end of our salvation, but the means as well.

Does this mean we have no responsibility to pray? Of course not. The responsibility for secondary causes that serve as means to the divine ends is still ours. But the point is that God's eternal ends are not at the mercy of our actions or lack of them. When we are engaged in prayer, something happens to us. We are changed by the experience. Prayer is a vital part of a living relationship we have with God. It is a kind of intercourse, or conversation, between two personal beings. One of these beings is immutable and omniscient; the other is mutable and lacking in perfect knowledge. In prayer God learns nothing new about us, but we are ever learning about Him.

In his novel *Honor Among Thieves*, Jeffrey Archer includes a poignant episode that involves two main characters of the story. Hannah Kopec is a beautiful young woman whose family was wiped out by missiles fired at Israel by Saddam Hussein. She enters rigorous training to become an agent of the Mossad. When she completes her training, she is sent to Paris to do espionage work in the Iraqi embassy. In the meantime an American professor of Yale University, Scott Bradley, is enlisted by the CIA to spy on Hannah. When Hannah is instructed by her superiors that she will be contacted by a Mossad agent in Paris, Bradley meets her and poses as that Mossad agent. In the ensuing days Hannah and Scott fall in love. Scott knows who Hannah is, but she does not know who Scott really is. As their relationship develops, Scott feels increasingly guilty about continuing the deception of the one he loves.

Meanwhile, Hannah is finally contacted by the real Mossad agent and discovers that Scott is an imposter. The Mossad does not know that Scott is working for their allies in the CIA and orders Hannah to kill him. Scott invites Hannah for dinner, secretly planning to confess to her that he has been living a lie and to reveal his true identity. She accepts his invitation, planning to use the occasion to obey the order to kill him.

When they meet for dinner Scott pours coffee for himself and for Hannah. Even though Hannah customarily does not use sugar in her coffee she asks Scott for some this time. When he goes to the kitchen to get the sugar bowl Hannah drops a lethal dose of poison in Scott's coffee. He returns with the sugar bowl, begins to drink his coffee, and then proceeds to confess all to Hannah. She listens in horror as she discovers she has just poisoned not only an ally but the man she loves more than anyone else in the world. In fairness to Jeffrey Archer I will not reveal here the end of the story but will use this scenario to point out that the story involves two people who know something (but not everything) about each other. Their relationship is affected by what they *don't* know about each other. Similarly, in prayer we are in a relationship in which one party knows something about the Other Party while the Other Party knows everything about the first party.

In prayer we have the opportunity to learn of the character of the Father. Indeed, prayer is one of the most effective means we have to discern the invisible hand of Providence. The more we understand the character of God, the easier it is for us to see His hand at work in our lives. This comes first from the self-revelation God gives in Scripture but also mightily in the experience of prayer. When we are praying in general we tend to see the work of Providence likewise "in general." When we pray specifically we begin to be overwhelmed by the specific answers to our prayer that vividly display His hand to us. By this our faith is strengthened, and our confidence in His Providence is intensified.

The Common Aspects of Prayer

It is customary to delineate the common aspects of prayer by the the acrostic ACTS. The A stands for adoration, the C stands for confession, the T stands for thanksgiving, and the S stands for supplication (or intercession). In each of these aspects, or elements, of prayer we are engaged in an exercise that is life-changing.

Adoration

No believer can spend much time in the adoration of God without being changed by the experience. We were created with the capacity for worship. Indeed, if we examine the prayer lives of the great saints we notice that the time they spend in adoration in their prayers is in direct proportion to their sanctification. Consider the psalms of David; these prayers are replete with adoration. The closer David draws to God, the more intense his expressions of praise and adoration become. What was true of David and the saints of church history will be true for us as well.

In adoration the focus of our attention is not upon ourselves or upon our own needs. Here the focus is on the glory and majesty of God. We are basking in His glory and delighting in His presence when we are engaged in authentic adoration. I think adoration is the most fulfilling dimension in prayer. Just as love letters between young lovers focus on the points of delight they find in their partners, so are lovers of God immersed in the praise of His perfections and excellency.

Confession

The cliché "confession is good for the soul" has become a cliché because it is true. In confession we loose our burden of unconfessed guilt. We do not tell God what has escaped His notice; He knows our sin, and we know that He knows it. But the act of telling it to Him is to acknowledge it for the sake of our own peace of mind. We are changed by the confession of our sin. We are not only changed in the sense that our status before God is changed. Nor are we changed merely by the forgiveness and cleansing that follow from it; we are changed in the very act of the confessing itself.

The relationship between adoration in prayer and confession is obvious. The more we contemplate the excellency of God in His perfect holiness the more cognizant we become of our own unworthiness. The more we learn of God the more we learn about ourselves. The more we learn about ourselves the more we realize we have to confess.

*

Thanksgiving

Just as God does not need our adoration to feel good about Himself or our confession to be aware of our sins, so He does not need the expression of our thanks to feel appreciated. We human beings are different: I do appreciate it when people thank me for things, and I know others feel the same sort of appreciation when I offer them my thanks. We need this kind of interchange among people, but God does not need it; nor is He in any way changed by it. Again, it is we who are changed by thanksgiving.

Thanksgiving and joy are not the same thing. They may be distinguished from one another, but they may not be separated. Joy evokes thanksgiving, and thanksgiving evokes joy. There is a symbiotic relationship between the two. When we contemplate the mercies we receive from the hand of Providence, which include the grace of His forgiveness, we are moved to gratitude. A grateful heart is a joyous heart. It is not an act of maudlin sentimentality to count one's blessings. To keep those blessings in mind is a fortress against despair and an overflowing fountain of joy.

Supplication

In supplication we bring our own needs and the needs of others before God. We are to make such supplications according to His law. God is not pleased or honored when we ask for things that He has prohibited by His law. This is an area that is fraught with peril. Professing Christians often ask God to bless or sanction their sin. They are even capable of telling their friends they have prayed about a certain matter and God has given them peace despite what they prayed for was contrary to His will. Such prayers are thinly veiled acts of blasphemy, and we add insult to God when we dare to announce that His Spirit has sanctioned our sin by giving us peace in our souls. Such a peace is a carnal peace and has nothing to do with the peace that passes understanding, the peace that the Spirit is pleased to grant to those who love God and love His law.

When we enter our supplications in behalf of others, we are participating in the priesthood of all believers and are doing what Luther described as "being Christ to our neighbor." Intercessory prayer imitates the work of Christ Himself, who ever intercedes for His people.

Just as redemption is a trinitarian work, so, in the economy of redemption, prayer is a trinitarian work. The Father commands us to pray. He hears our prayers. He answers our prayers. But when we pray to Him we are not alone in our endeavor. The Father has appointed the Son to be our Intercessor. Christ enhances the efficacy of our prayers by mediating them to the Father by His own intercession. That is why we pray through Christ and in His name.

Likewise, in the economy of redemption the Holy Spirit is sent to us both by the Father and the Son to assist us in prayer. He aids us in preparing our souls to pray in a proper attitude and to pray according to the Father's will. The more we seek the assistance of the Spirit the more answers to prayer we see simply because we are praying within the will of the Father. The Spirit Himself is invisible to our eyes, but His work illumines our minds to the secret things of God.

The Providence of God is our fortress, our shield, and our very great reward. It is what provides courage and perseverance for His saints. This book but scratches the surface of the mysteries that are hidden in His great providence. May it function as a stimulus to delve deeper into the matter for all who read it.